TOKYO CINEROTIX
100 SCENES FROM CLASSIC JAPANESE SEXPLOITATION CINEMA

真☆爆 SHINBAKU

TOKYO CINEROTIX
EDITED BY KAGAMI JIGOKU KOBAYASHI
ISBN : 978-1-84068-342-4
PUBLISHED BY SHINBAKU BOOKS 2024
COPYRIGHT © FABBRICA SODOMA 2024
THANKS TO: BLACK GAS ENTERTAINMENT
ALL WORLD RIGHTS RESERVED

FOREWORD

Nudity has featured in Japanese "exploitation" cinema since the late 1950s, in films like **Onna shinju-ô no fukushû** (1956) and others featuring naked girl divers. Female nudity as an adjunct to violence, blood-letting and horror first appeared in the landmark **Kyûjûkyû-honme no kimusume** (1959), and continued in the 1960s with the likes of **Onibaba** and **Moju**. Meanwhile, the purely erotic genre itself – known as "pink cinema" in Japan – began to emerge with stag movies such as **Nikutai no ichiba** in 1962. The pink genre finally grabbed the headlines with Tetsuji Takechi's **Hakujitsumu** (1964), which caused much embarrassment by opening at the same time as the Tokyo Olympics.

Soon, certain filmmakers began to utilise the emerging sex film format as a vehicle for political statement; for example, Takechi with **Kuroi yuki** (1965), Yoshishige Yoshida with **Erosu purasu gyakusatsu** (1969), and renegade director Koji Wakamatsu who made the outstanding "pink" films of the 1960s: weird, violence- and sex-filled quasi-political trips which remain classics of underground cinema, such as **Okasareta hakui**, **Shojo geba geba**, and **Tenshi no kôkotsu**.

Wakamatsu, like so many other '60s directors, had cut his teeth with the Nikkatsu Company – the doyen of Japanese exploitation film producers. It was Nikkatsu who, in 1971, invented the ultimate pink movie genre: the Roman Porno. From the very first film, **Danchizuma: Hirusagari no jôji**, this very adult and stylish sexploitation genre was a wild success, continuing until the end of the 1970s, at which point video started to take over the adult market. Using the most famous and beautiful actresses, a slew of extremely talented directors, and marked by a uniquely Japanese streak of cruelty and perversity, the Roman Porno represents a pinnacle in adult cinema. In the pages that follow you will see stills from dozens of these movies; as well as many many others from the various film studios who strove to emulate Nikkatsu. **TOKYO CINEROTIX** is a testament to the girls who bared all in these ground-breaking erotic productions, and is published as a tribute both to them and to an age of cinema that will never be repeated.

百合族2 映倫

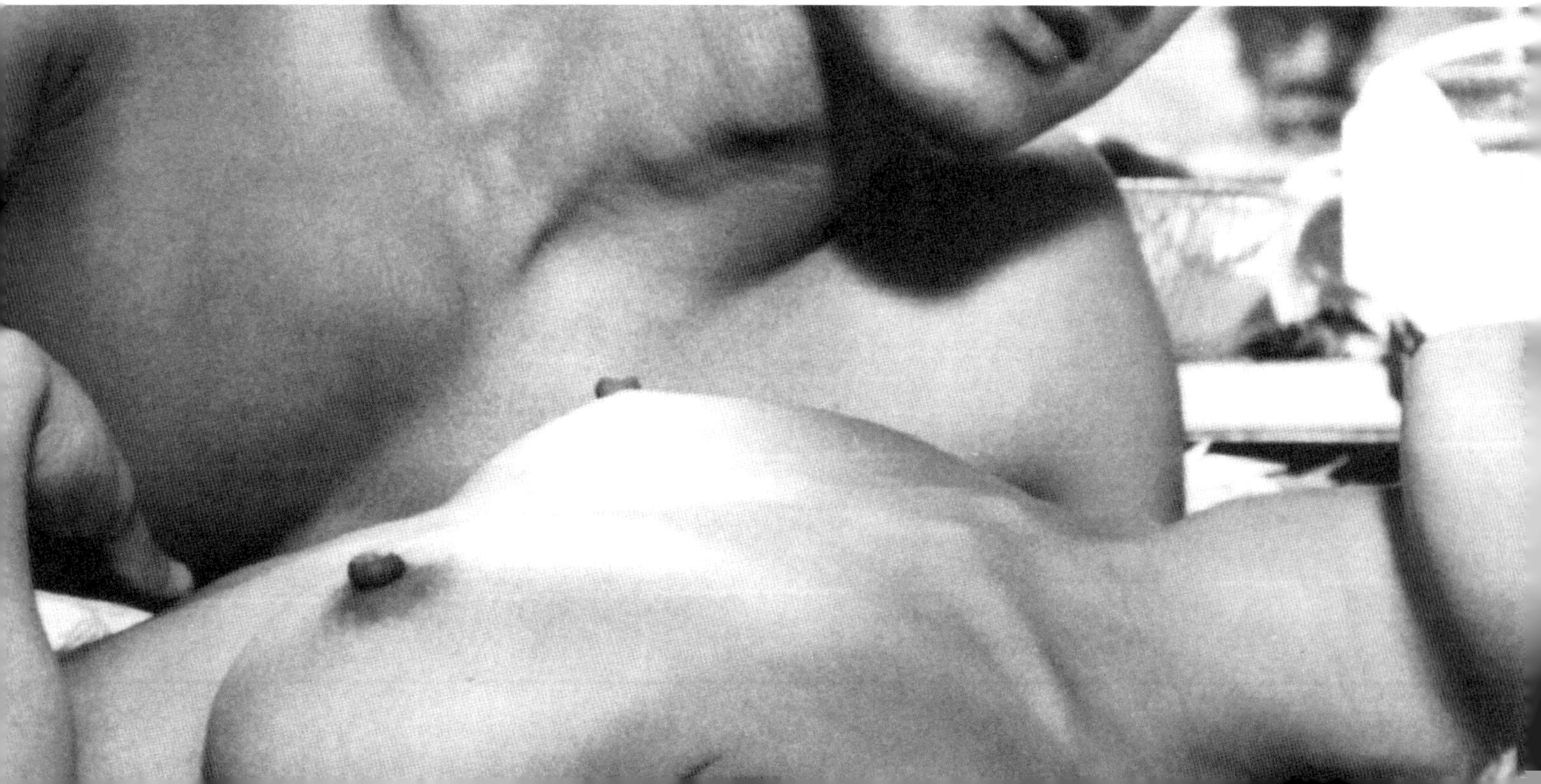

痴漢戯 [映倫]

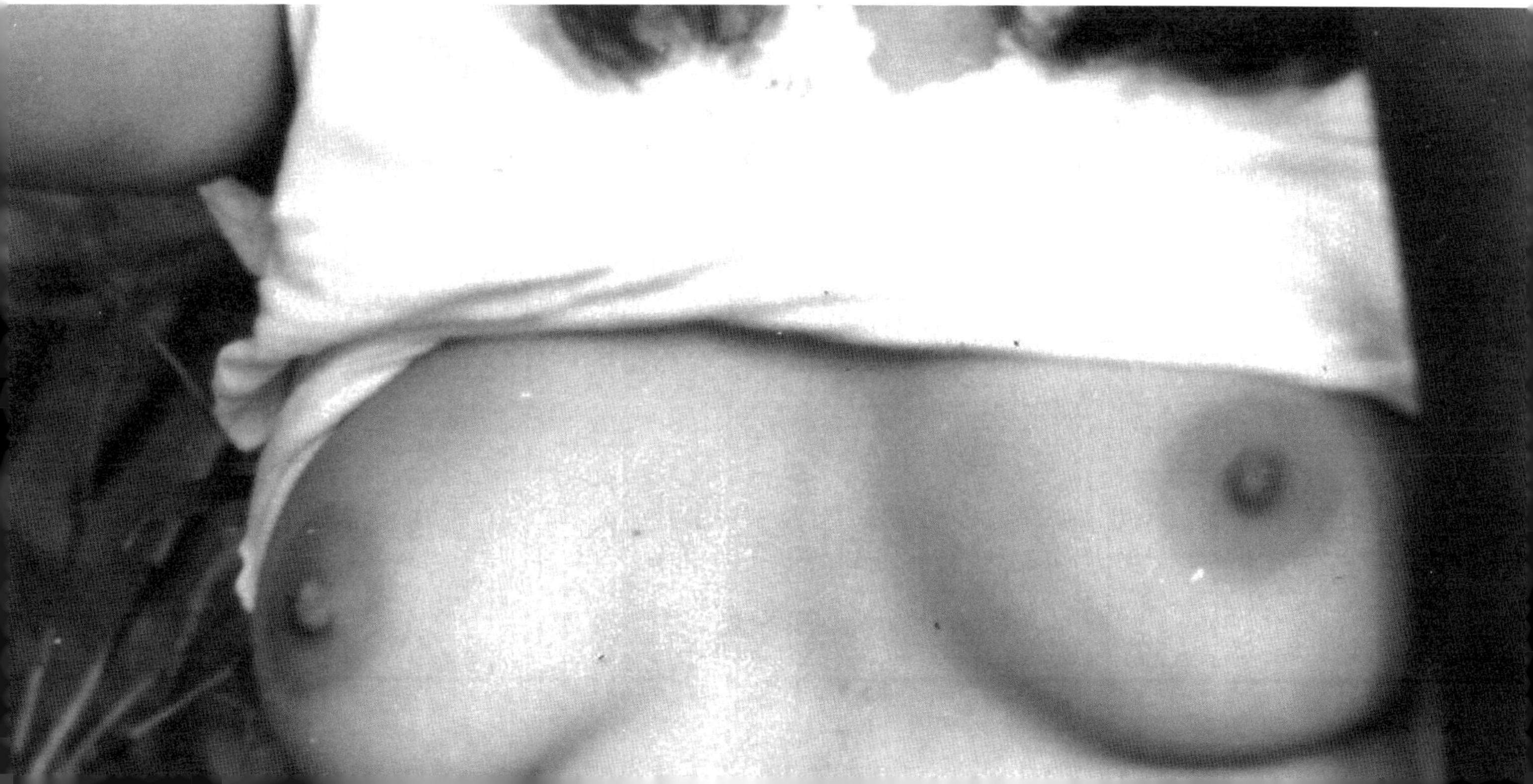

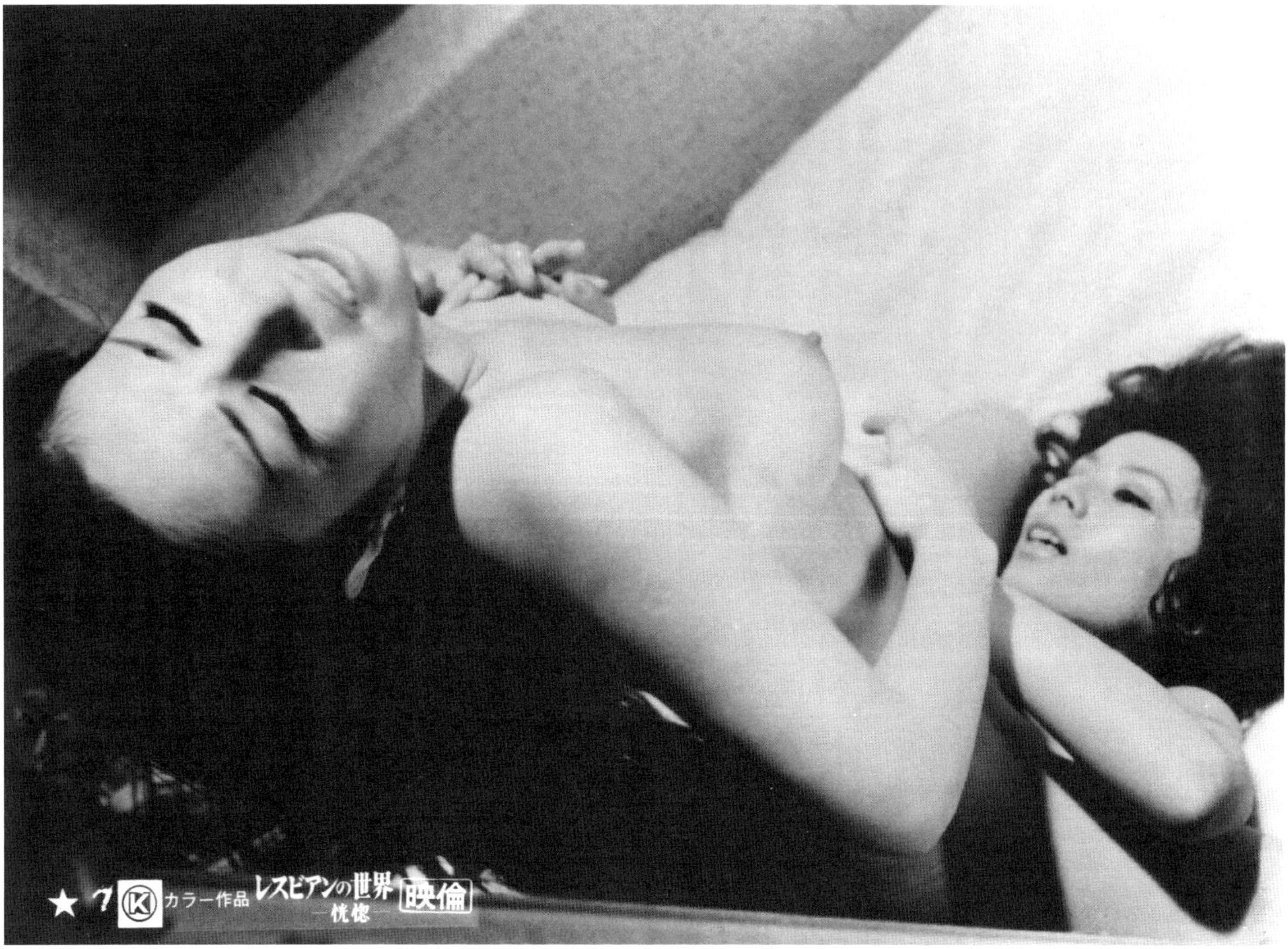

7 Ⓚ カラー作品 レスビアンの世界―恍惚 映倫

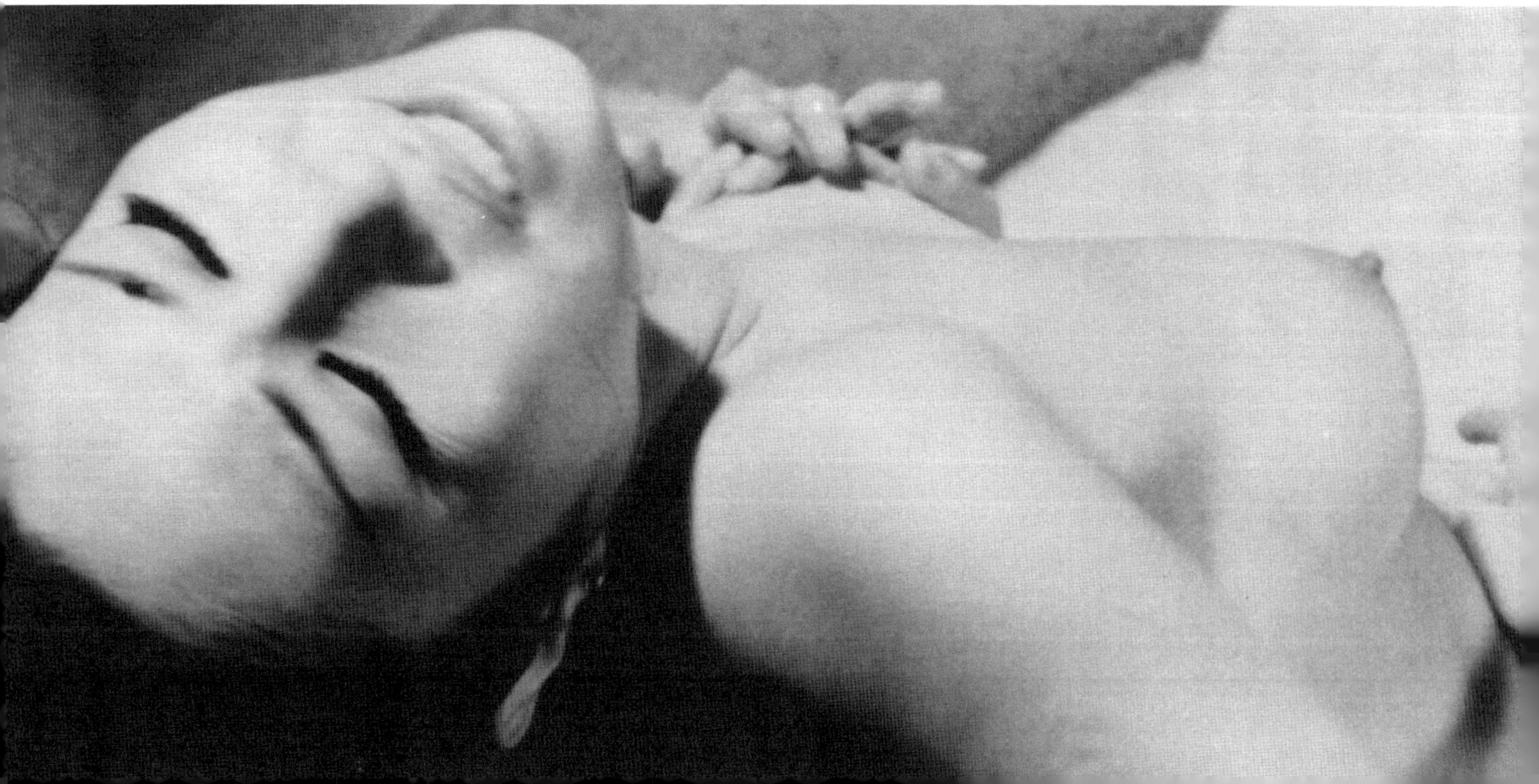

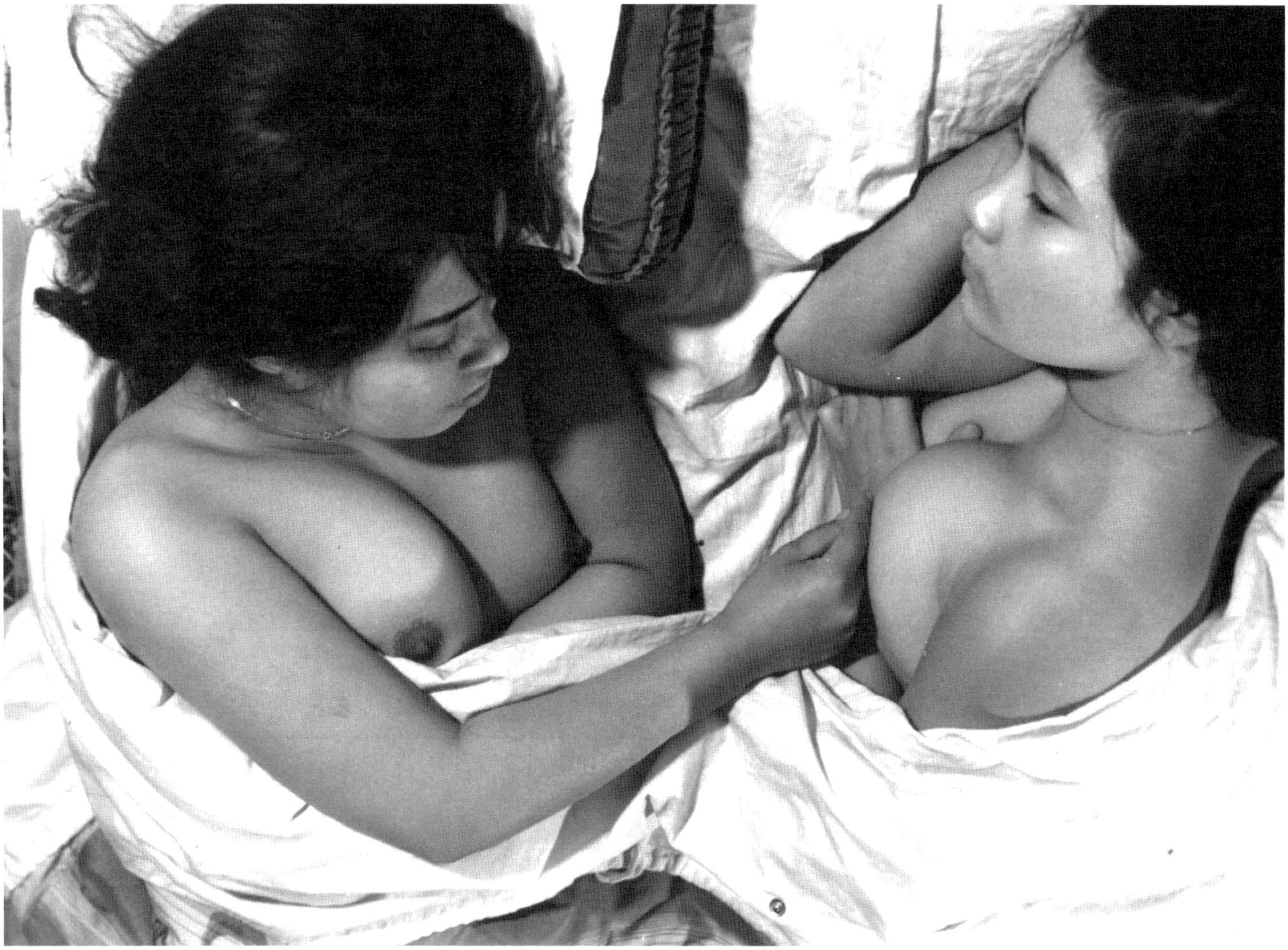

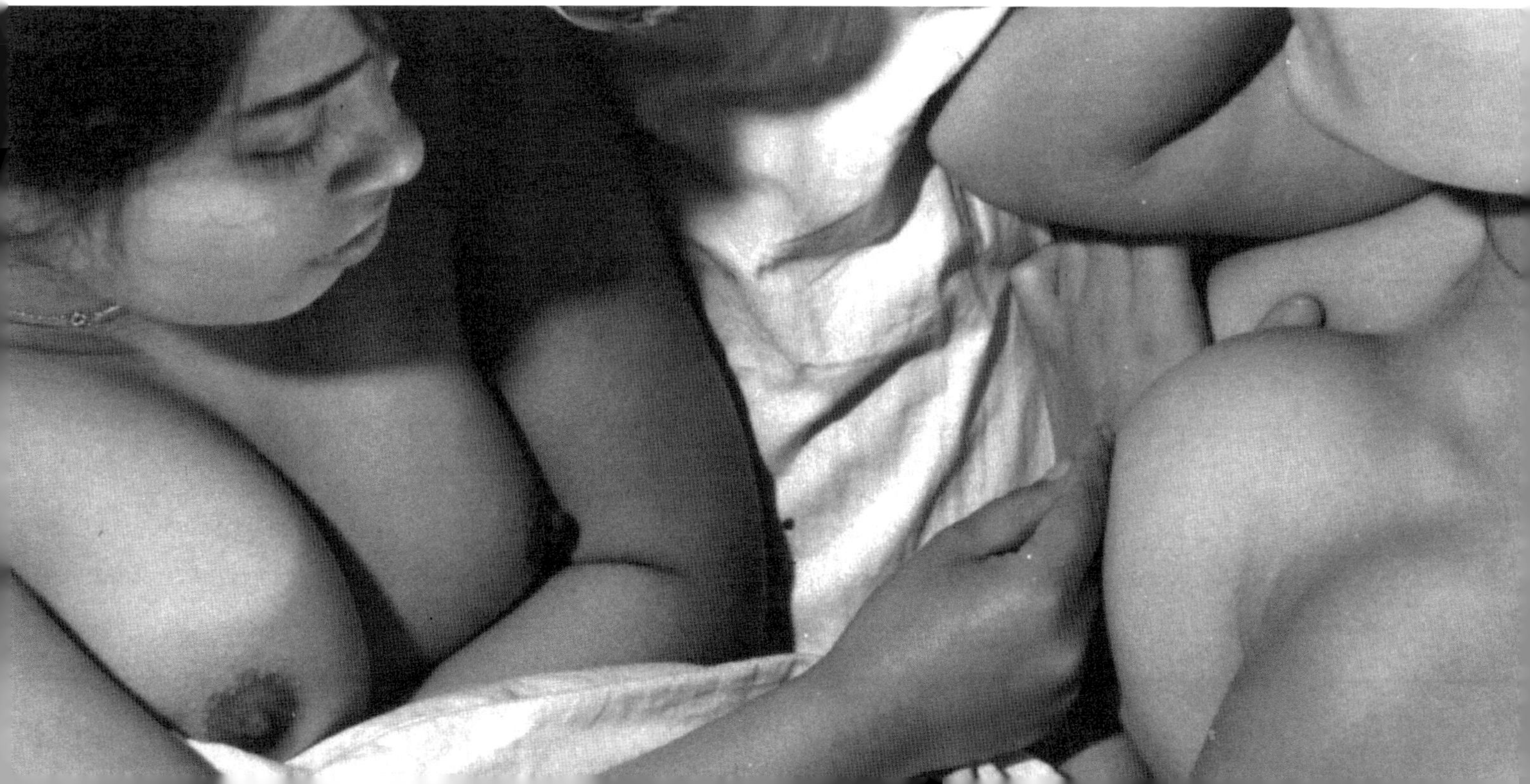

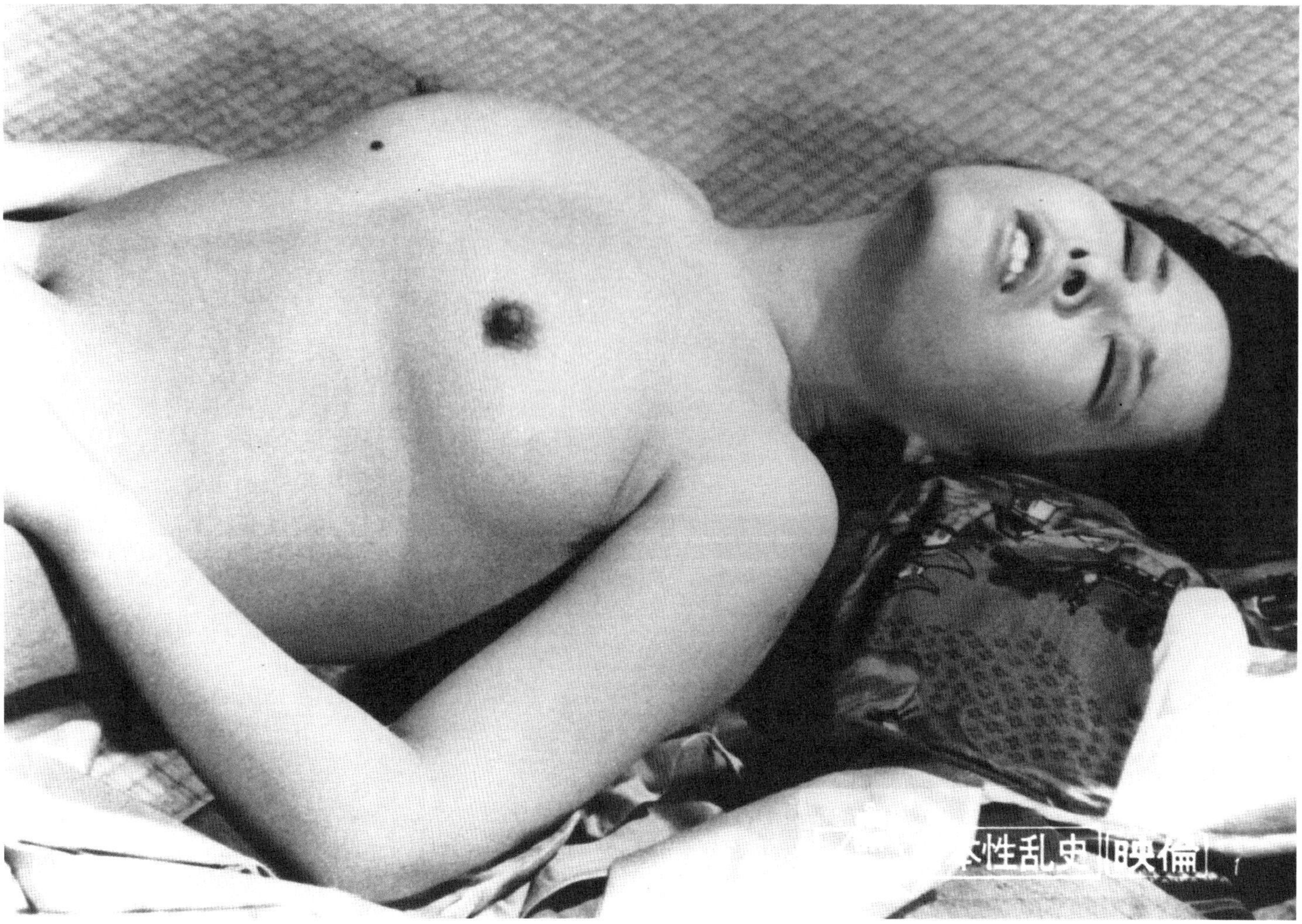

性乱史「映倫」

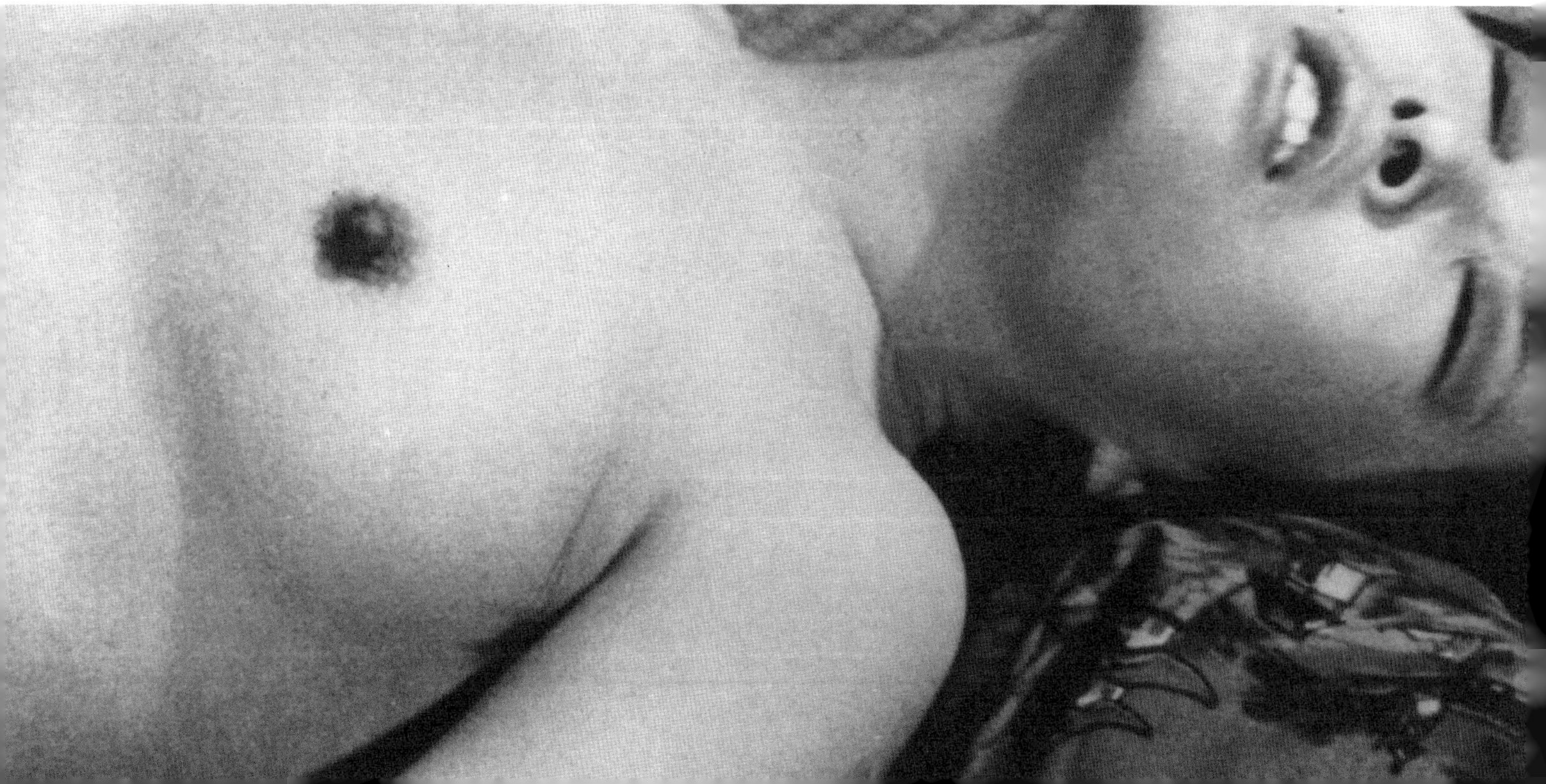

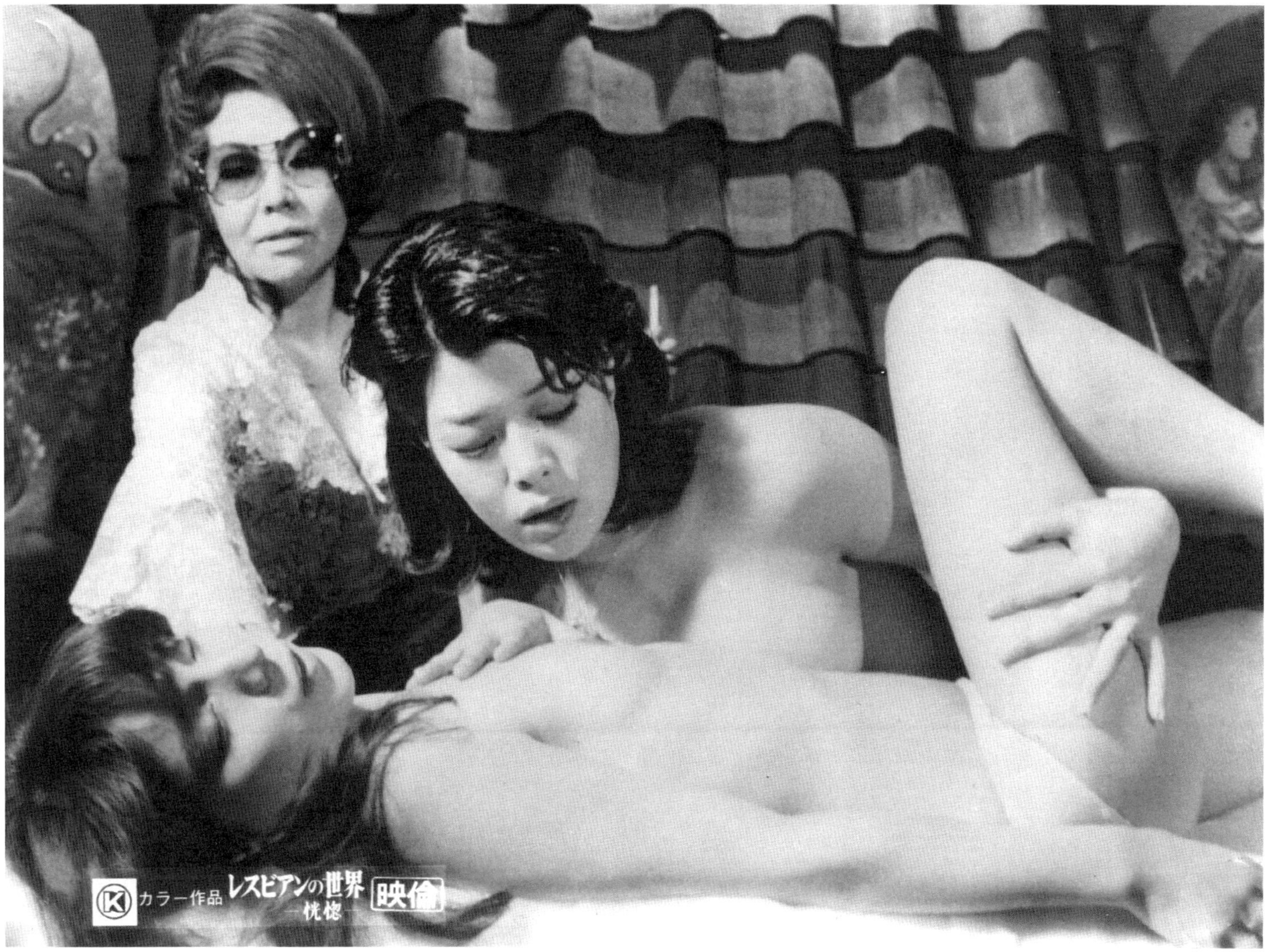

カラー作品 レスビアンの世界 —恍惚— 映倫

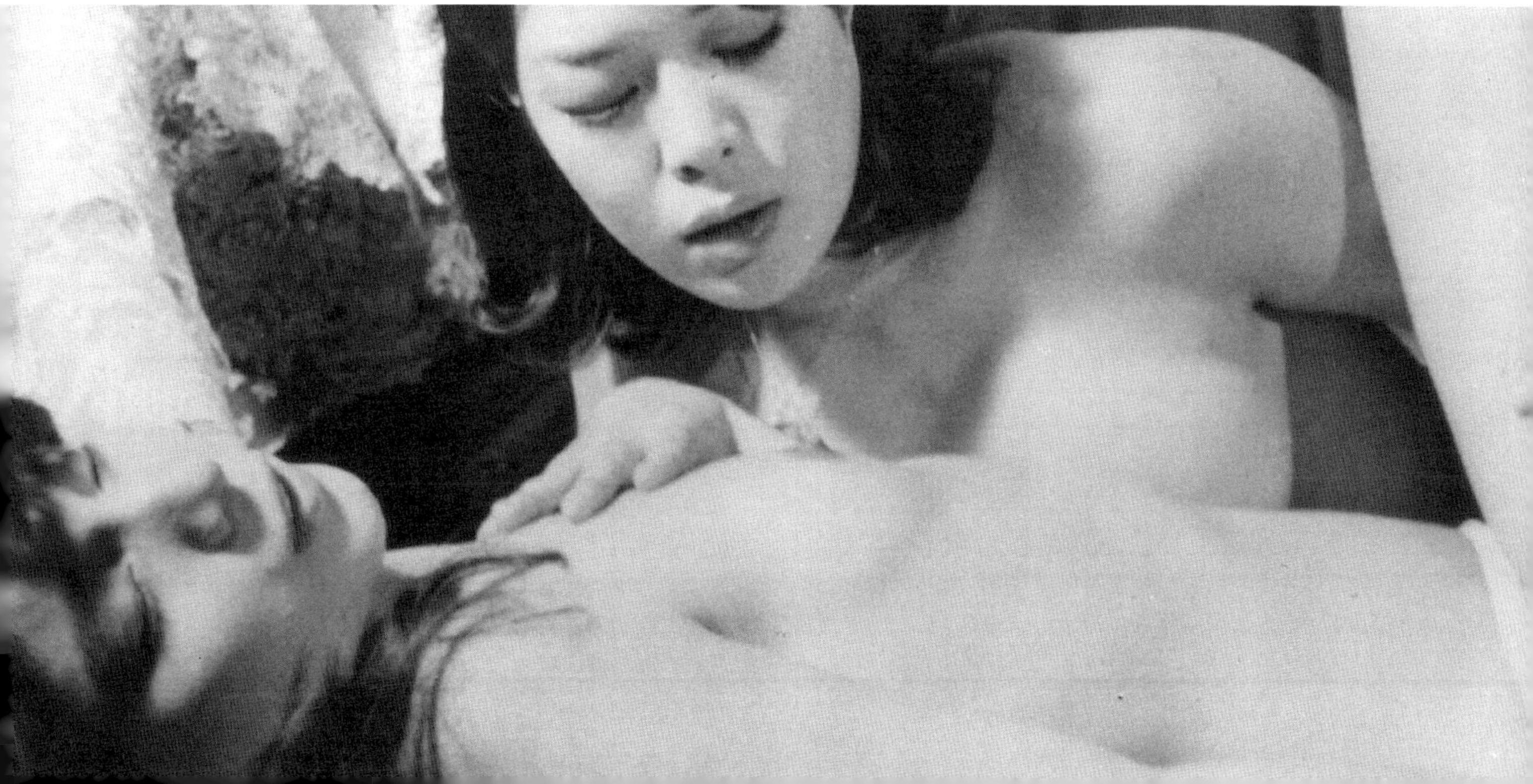

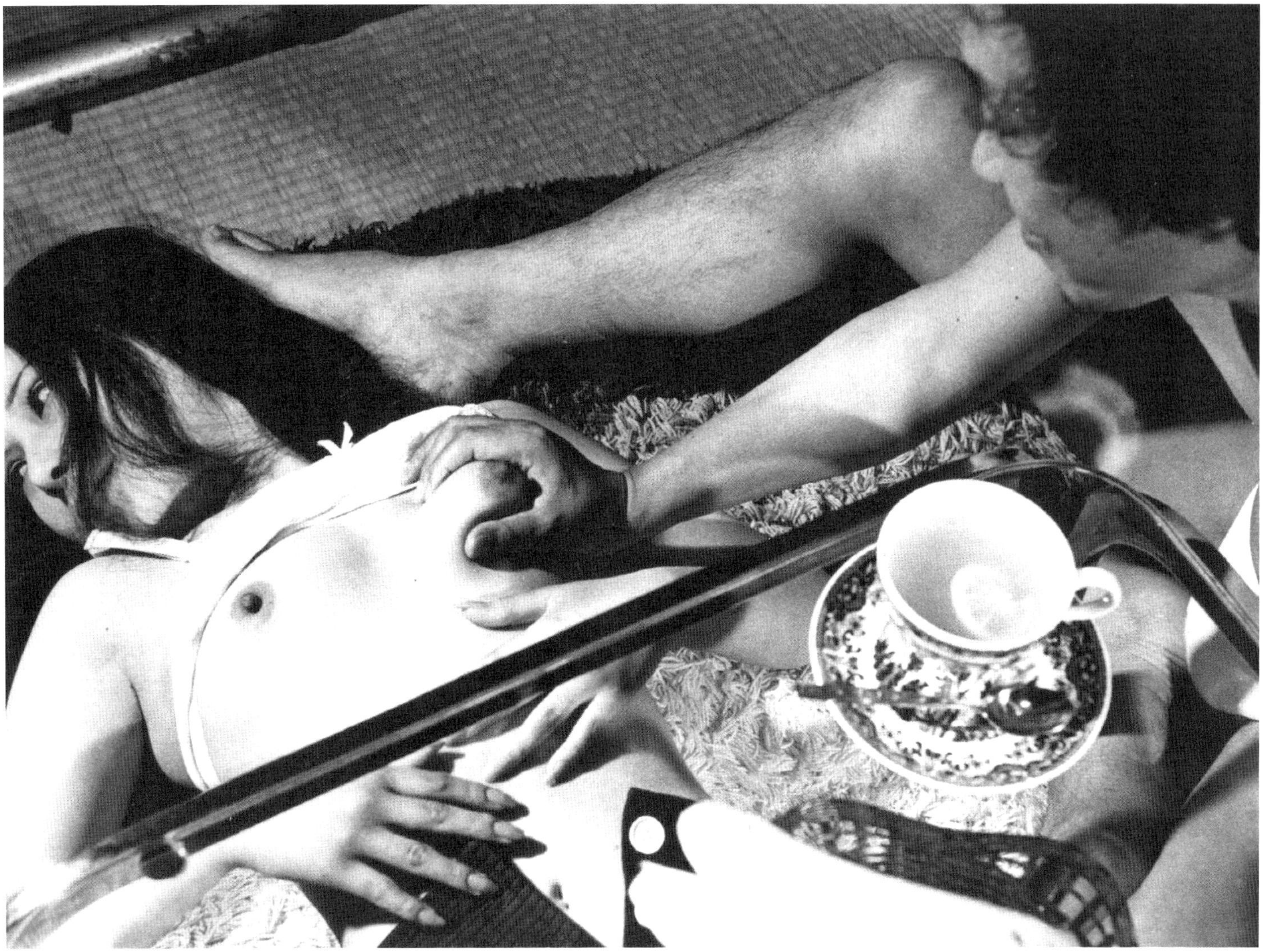

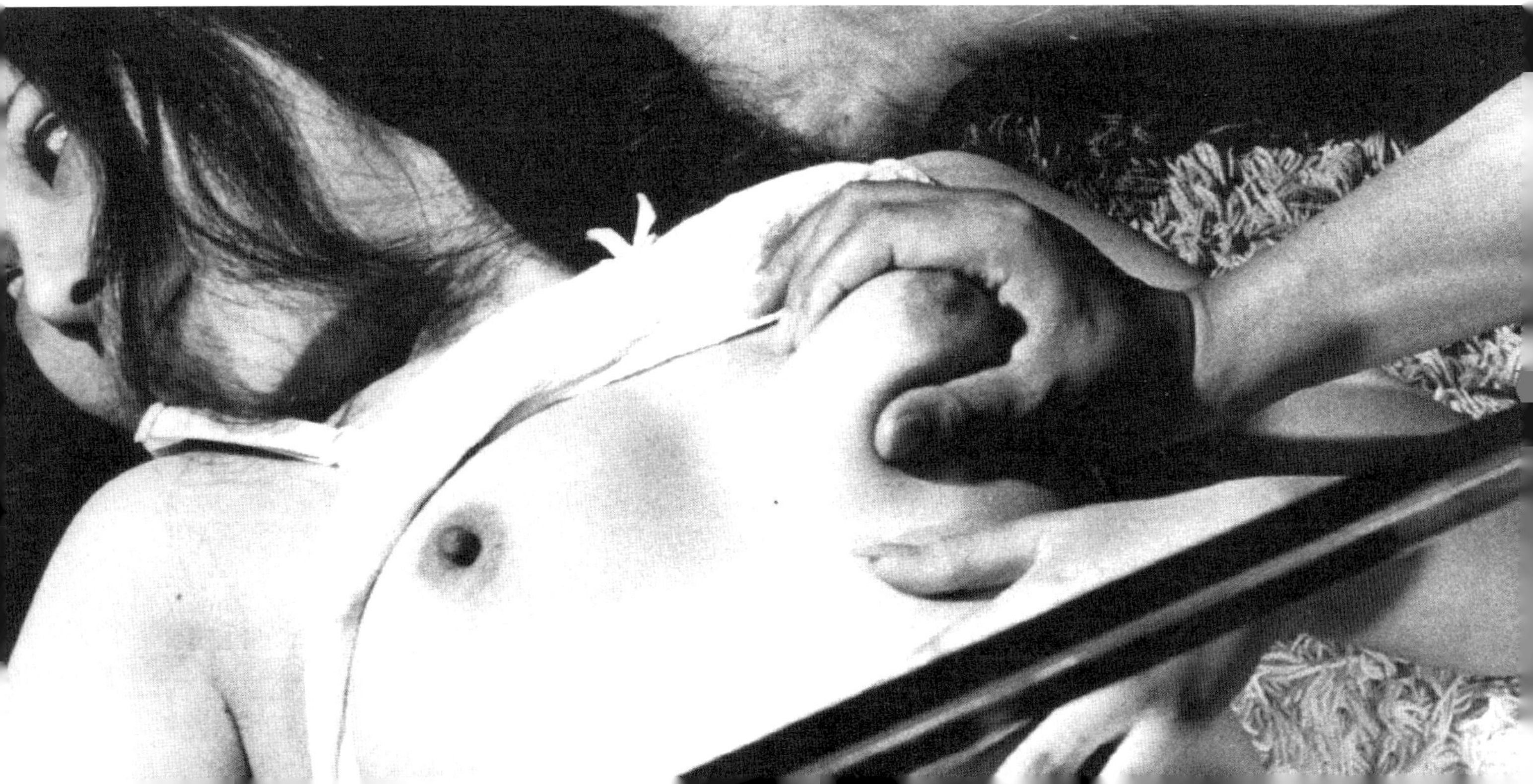

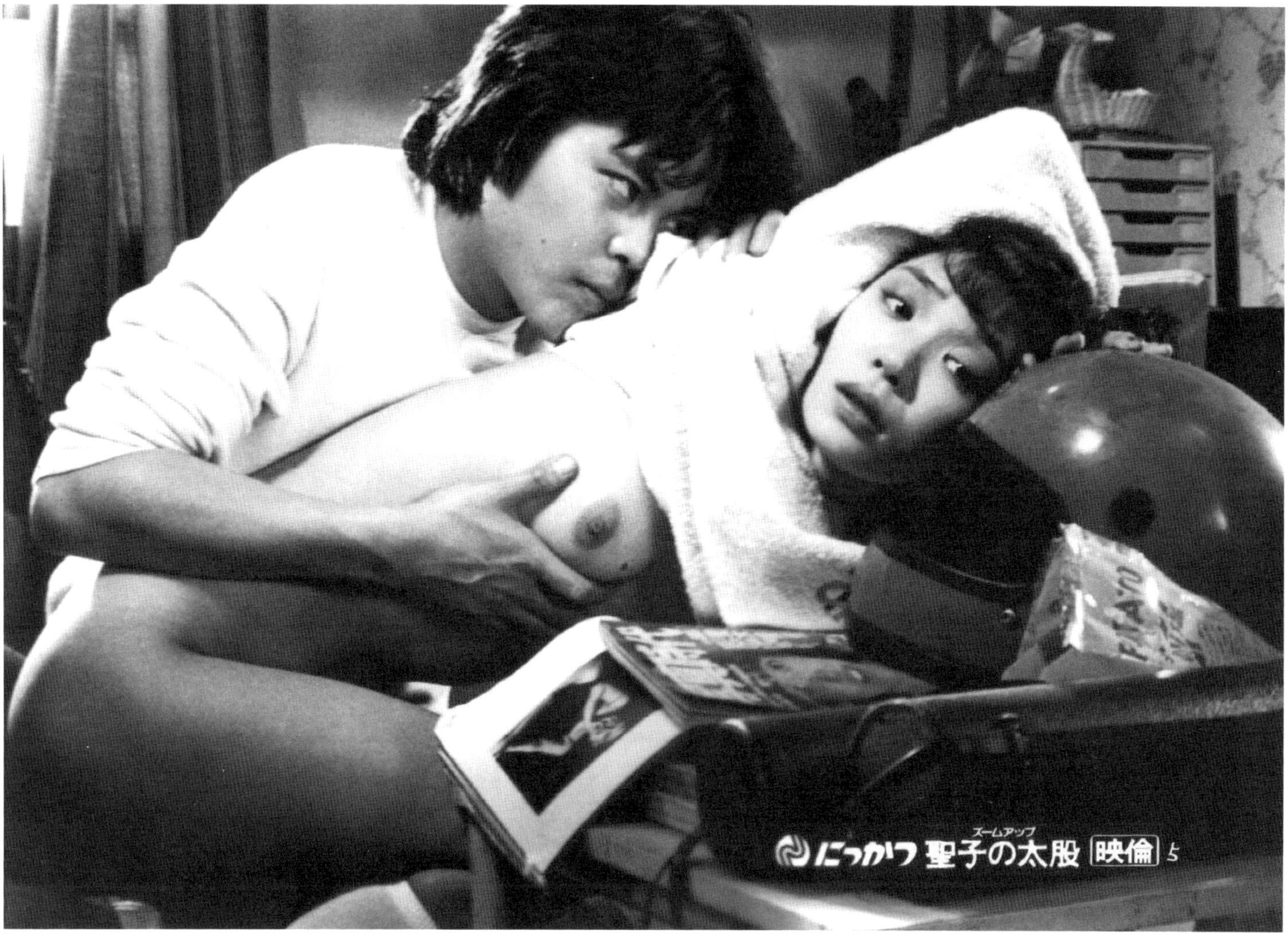

にっかつ ズームアップ 聖子の太股 映倫 5

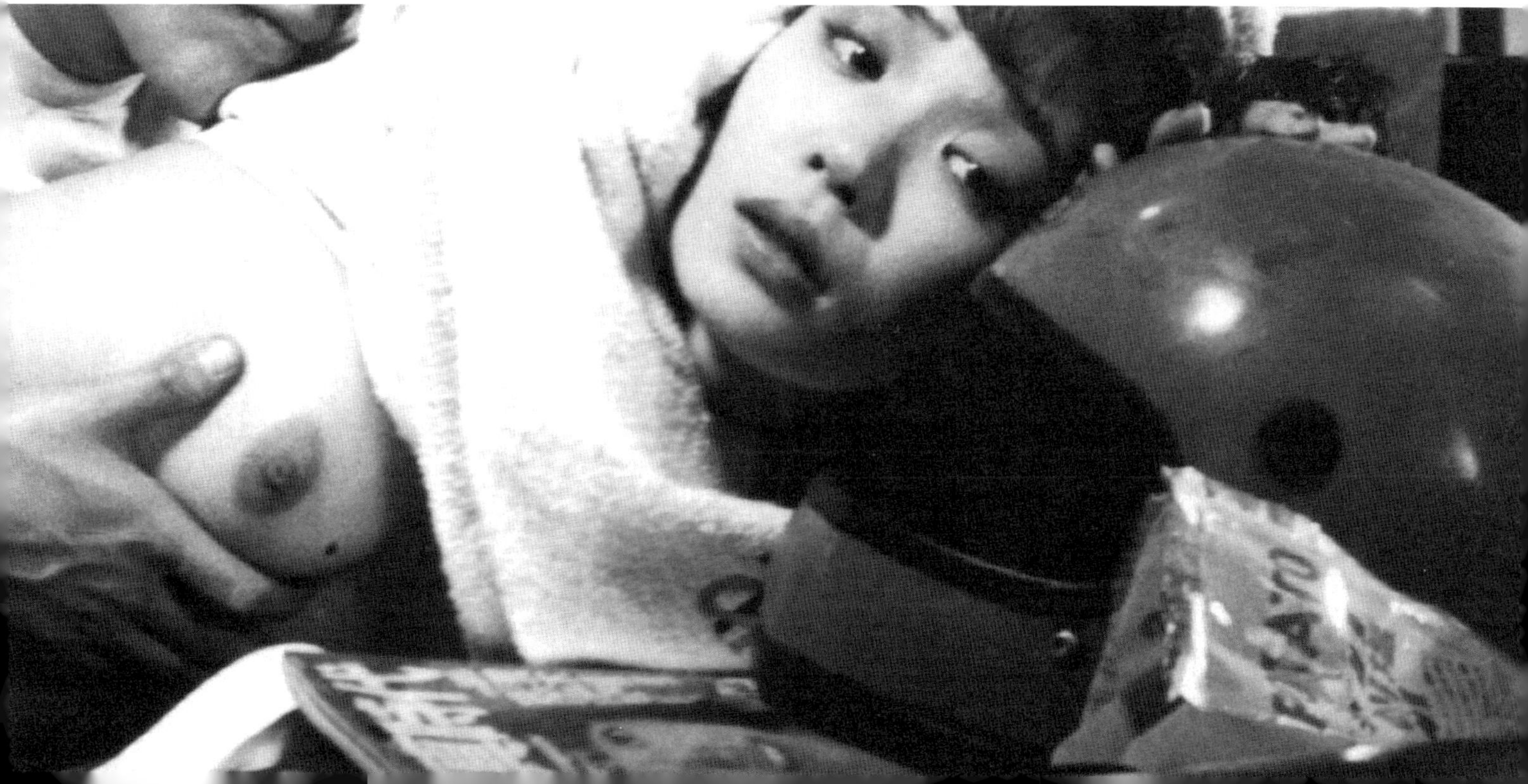

カラー作品 襲う!! 映倫

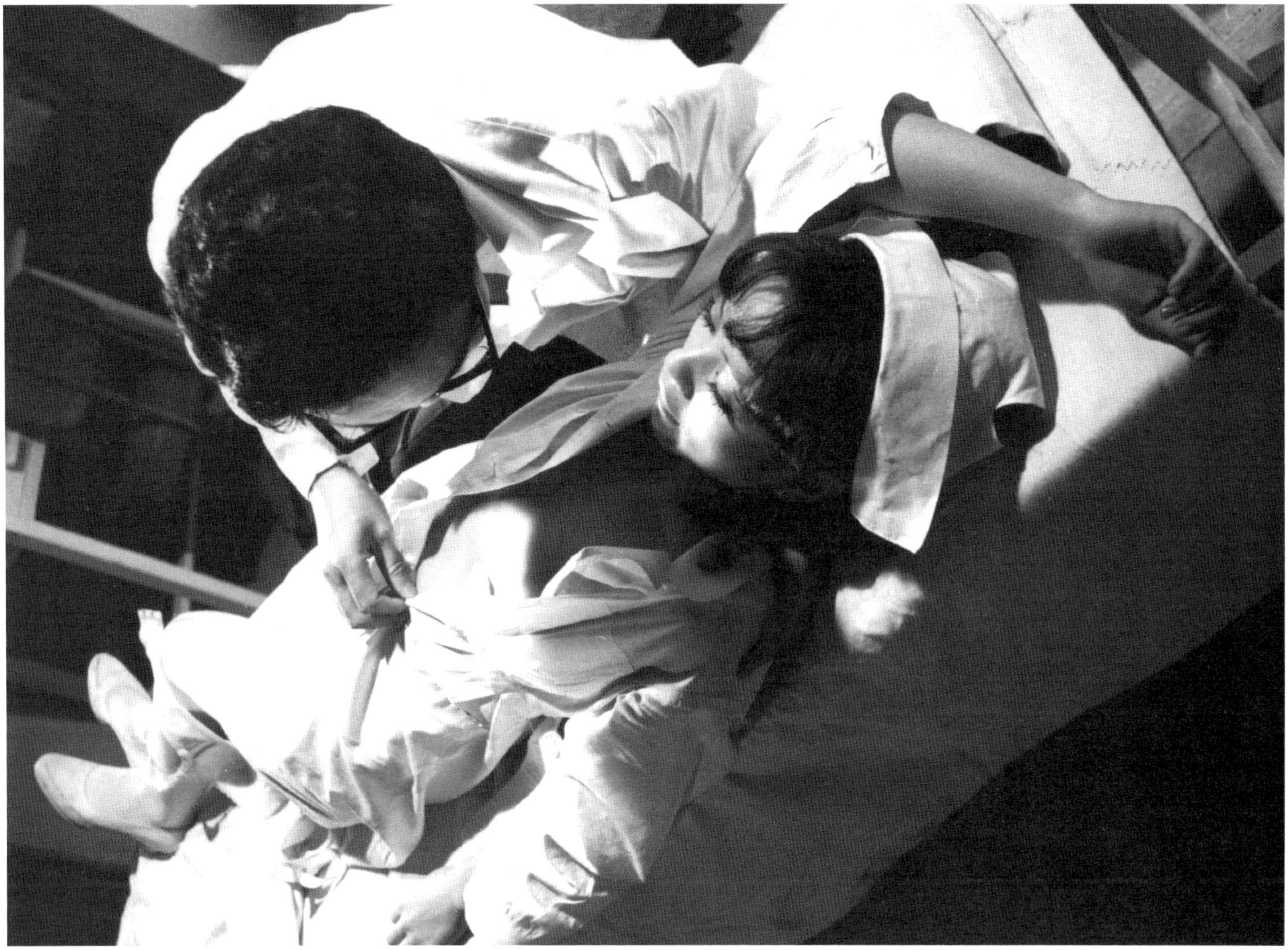

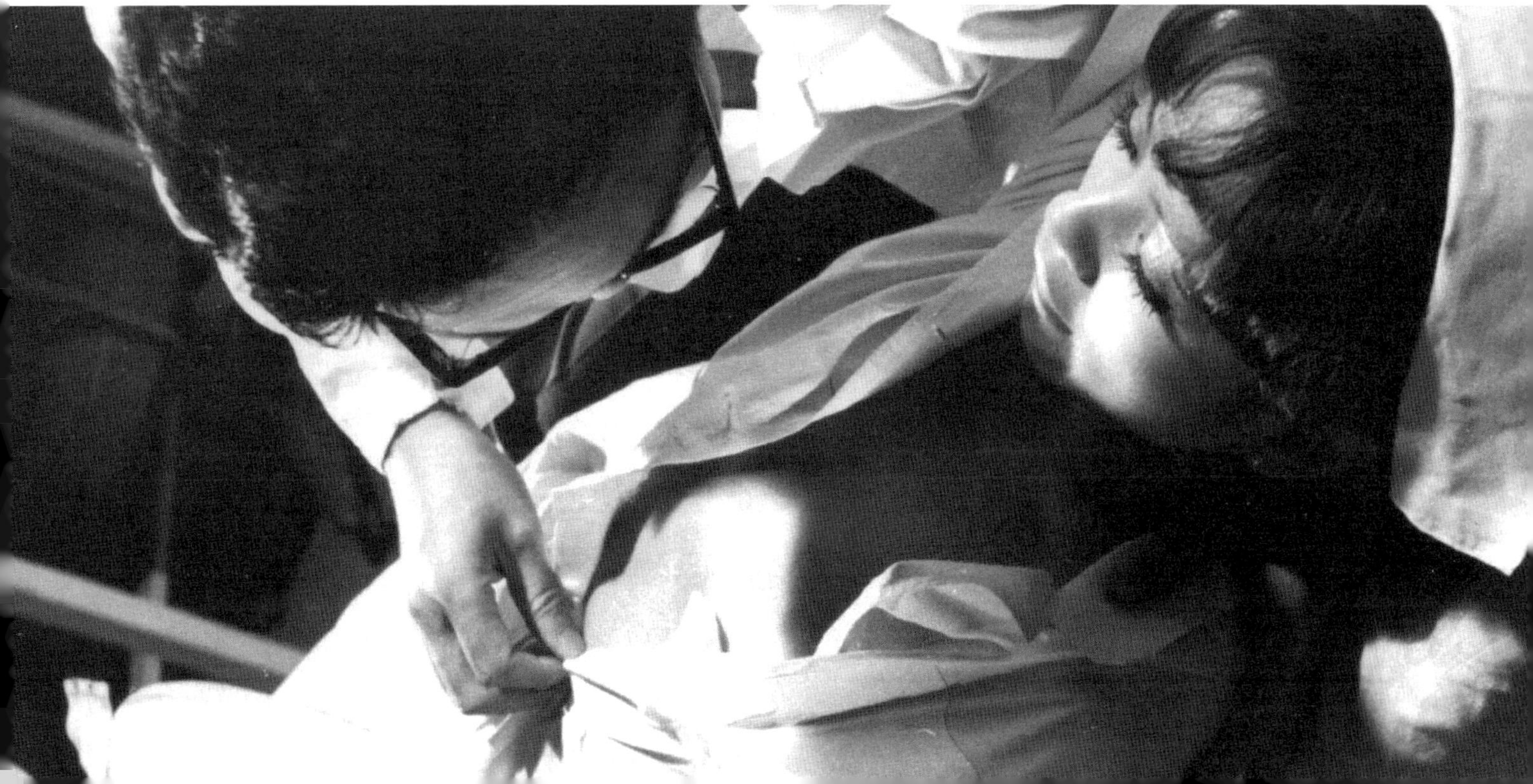

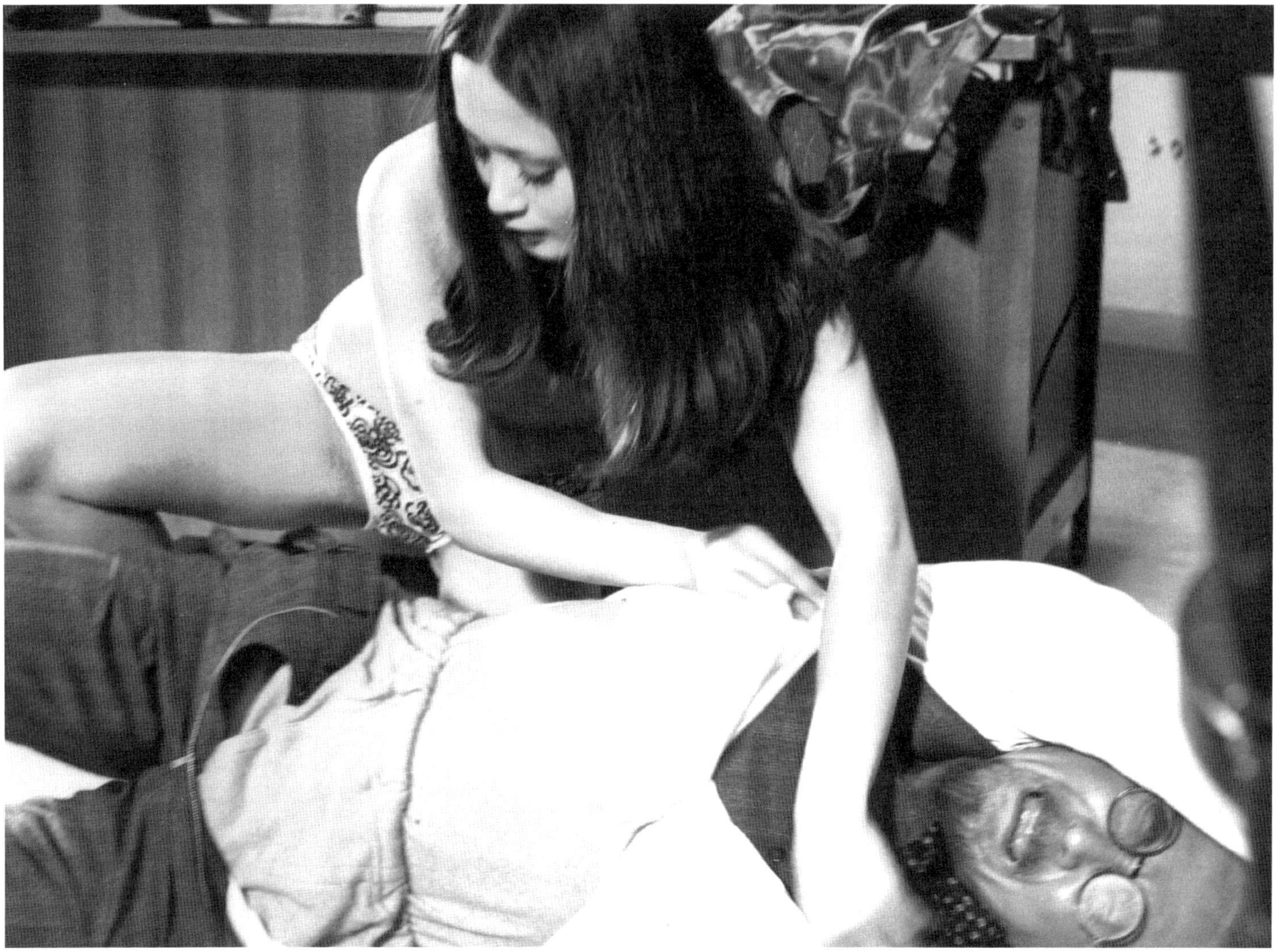

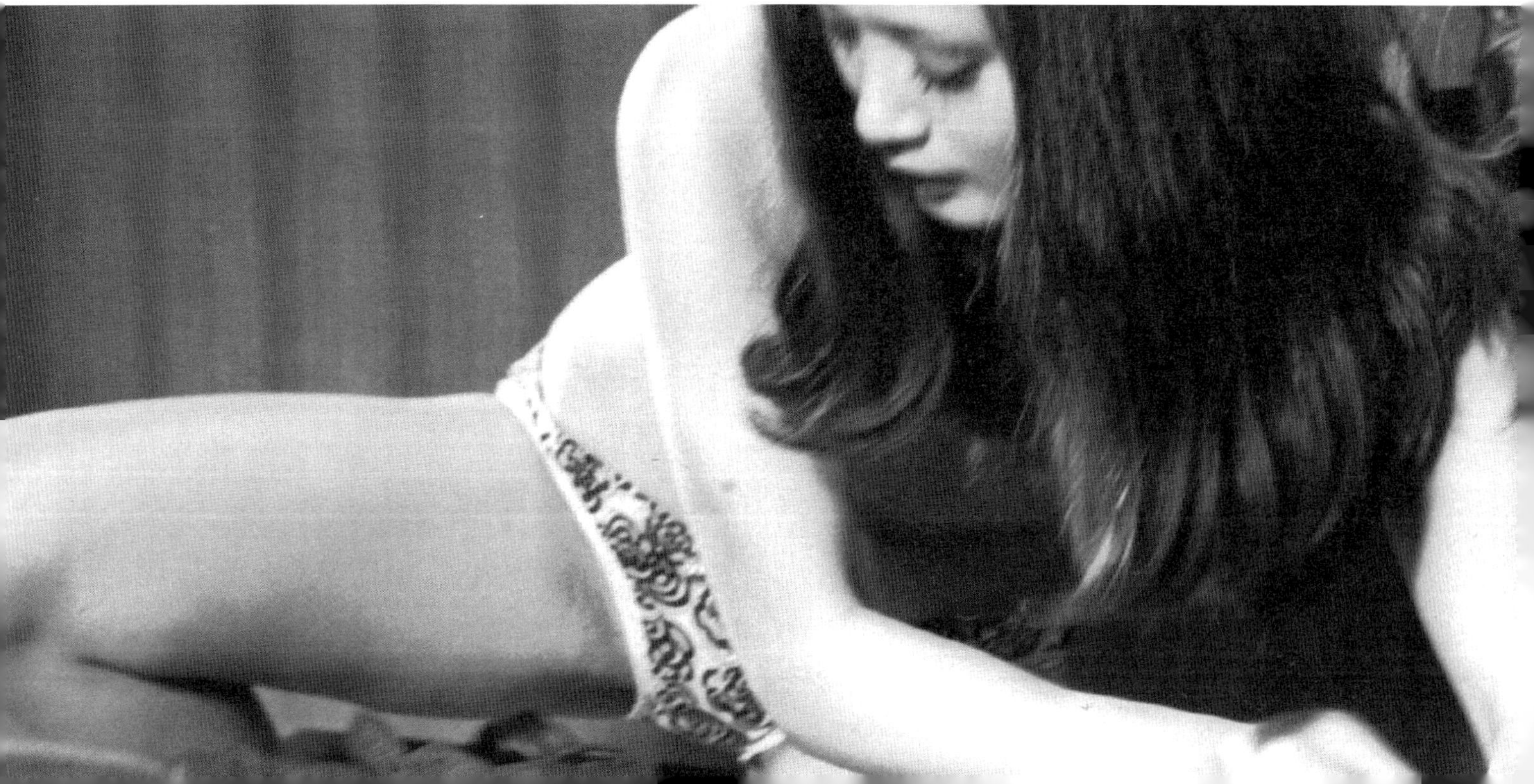

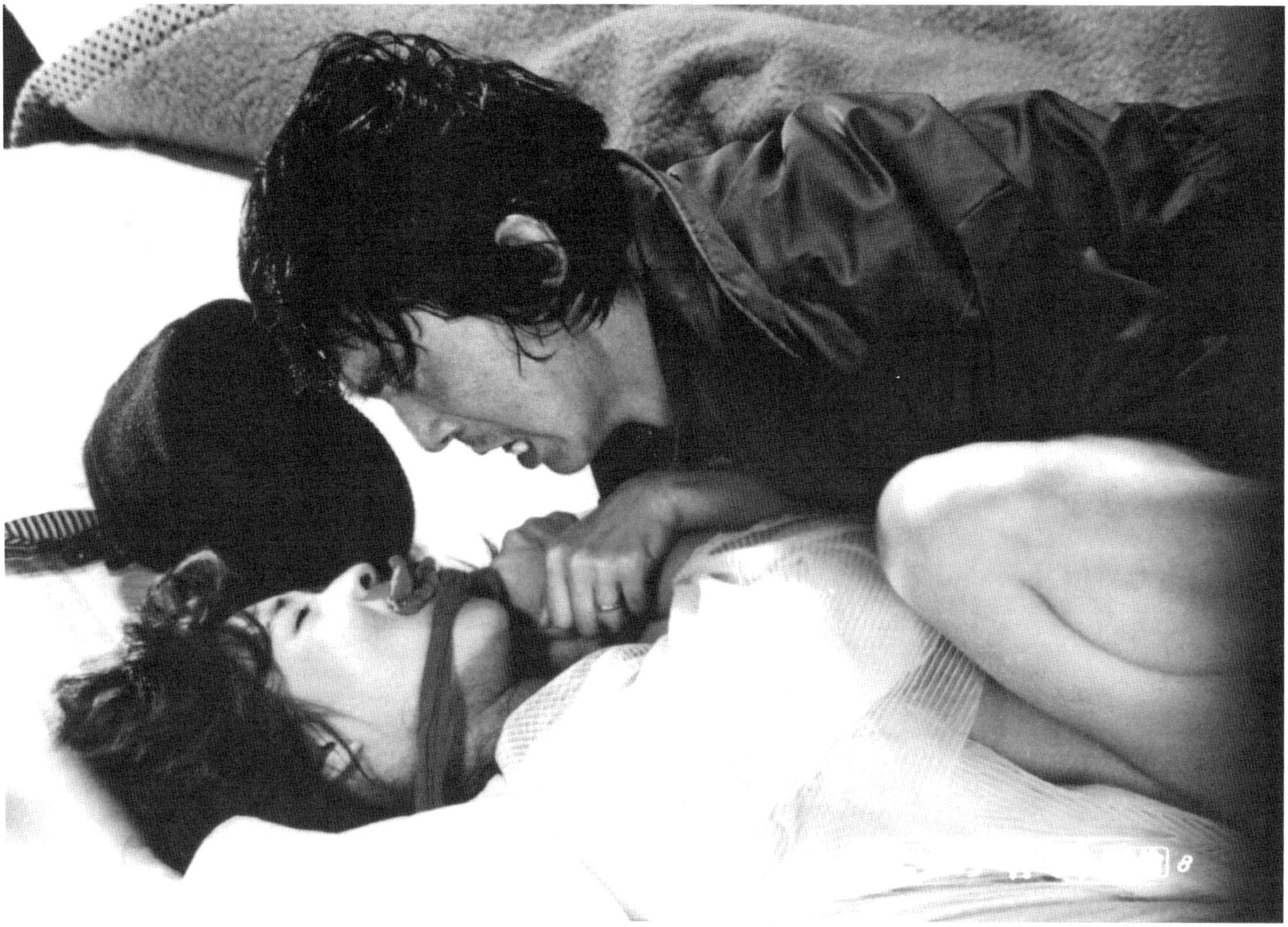

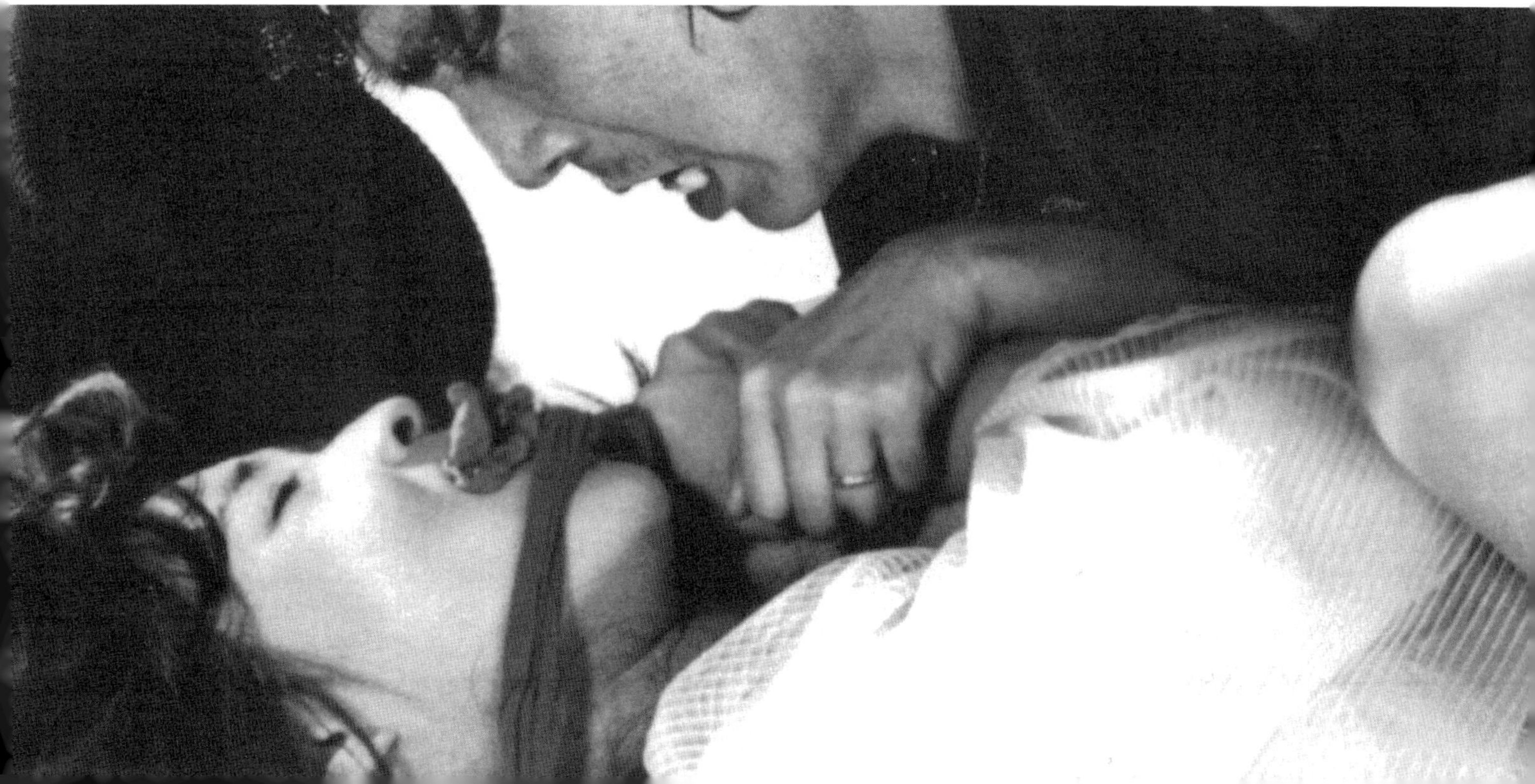

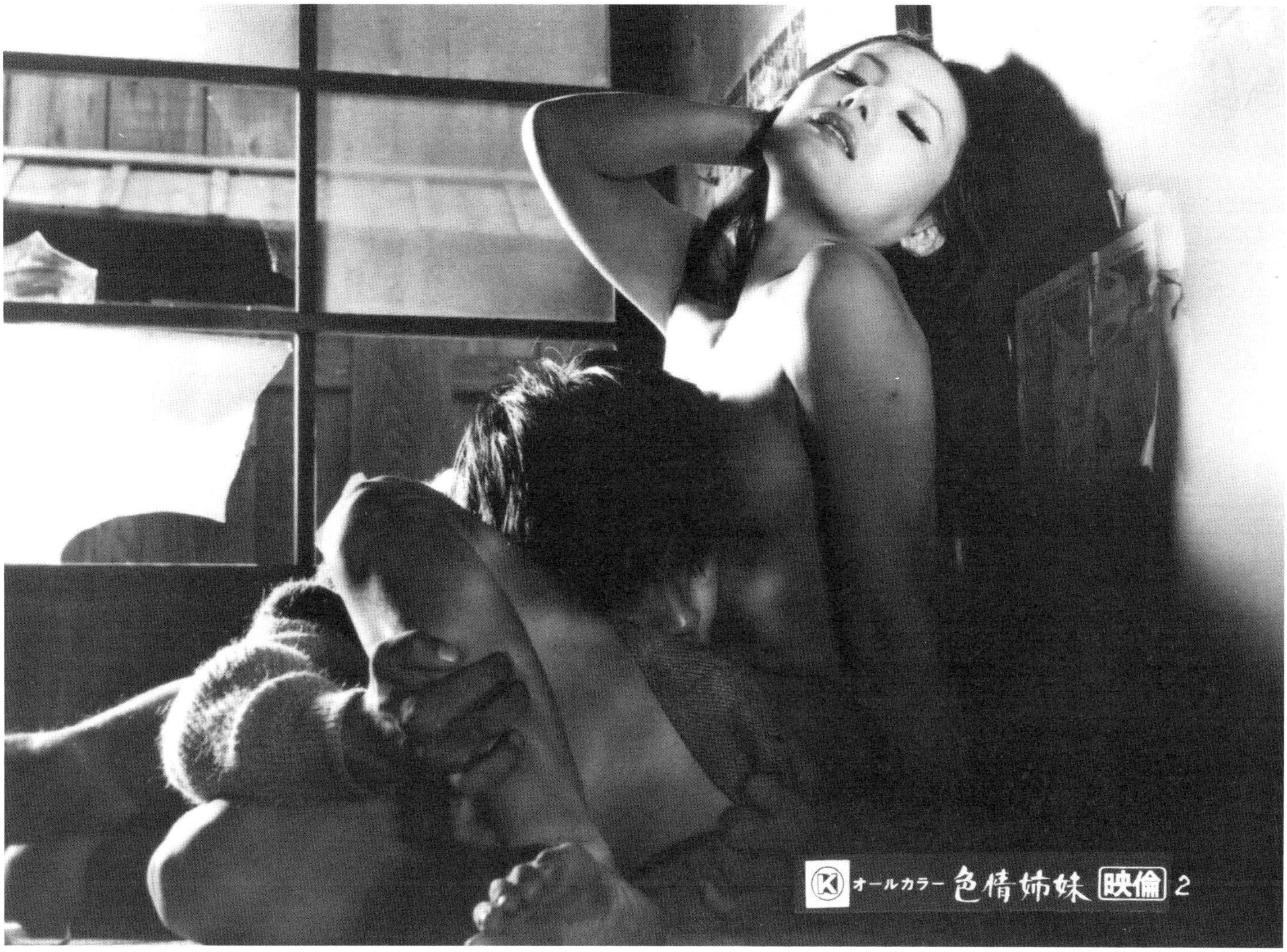

オールカラー 色情姉妹 映倫 2

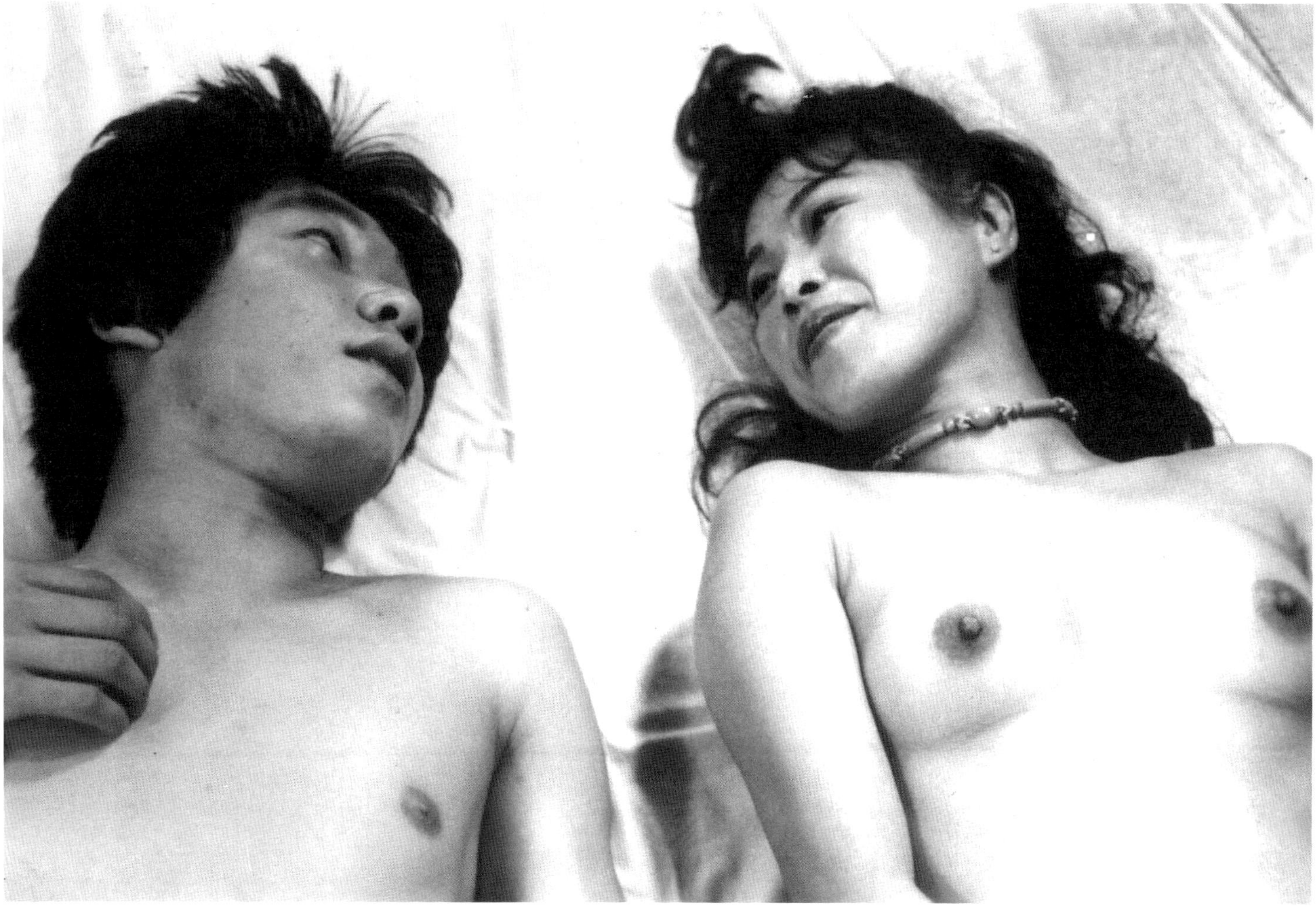

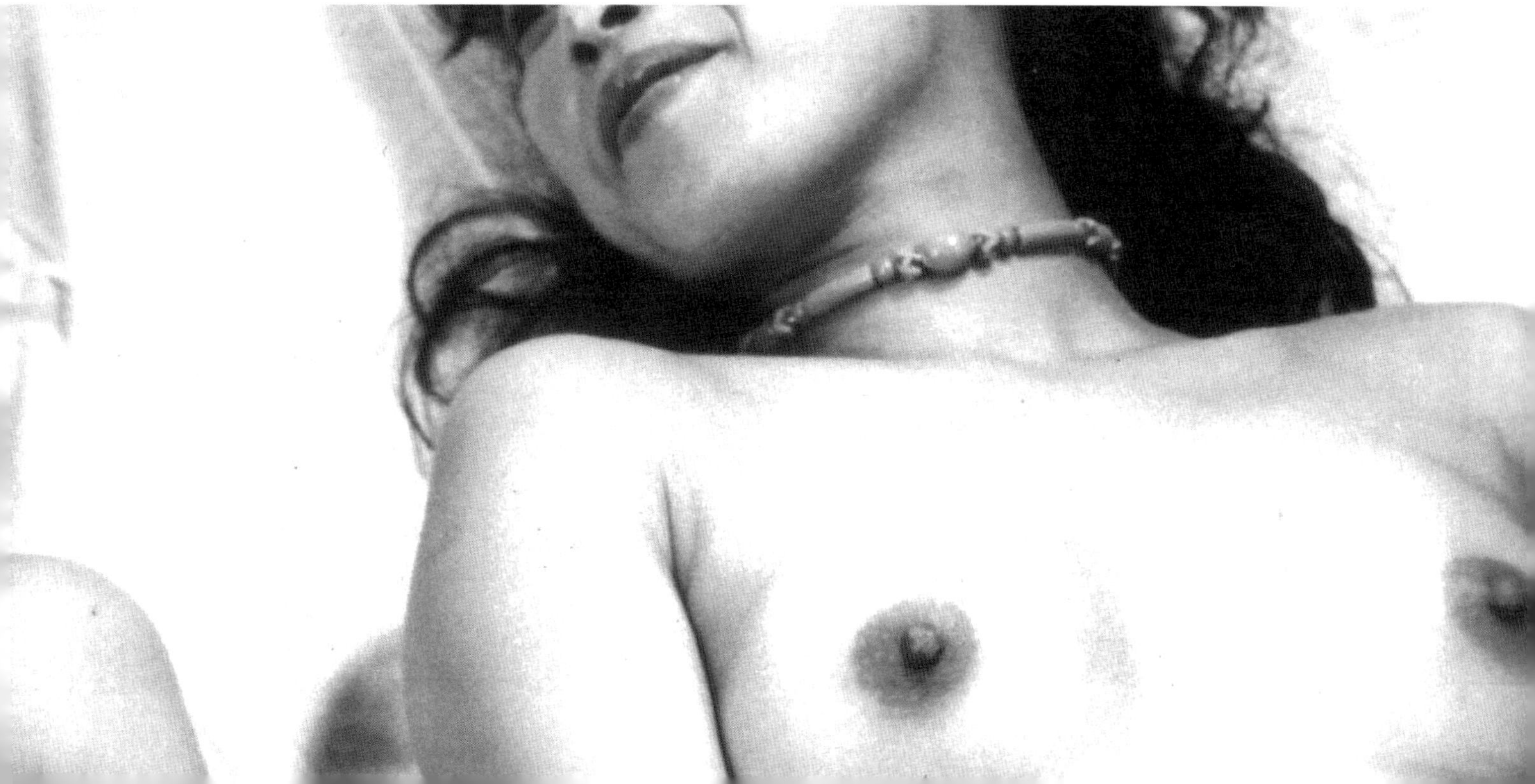

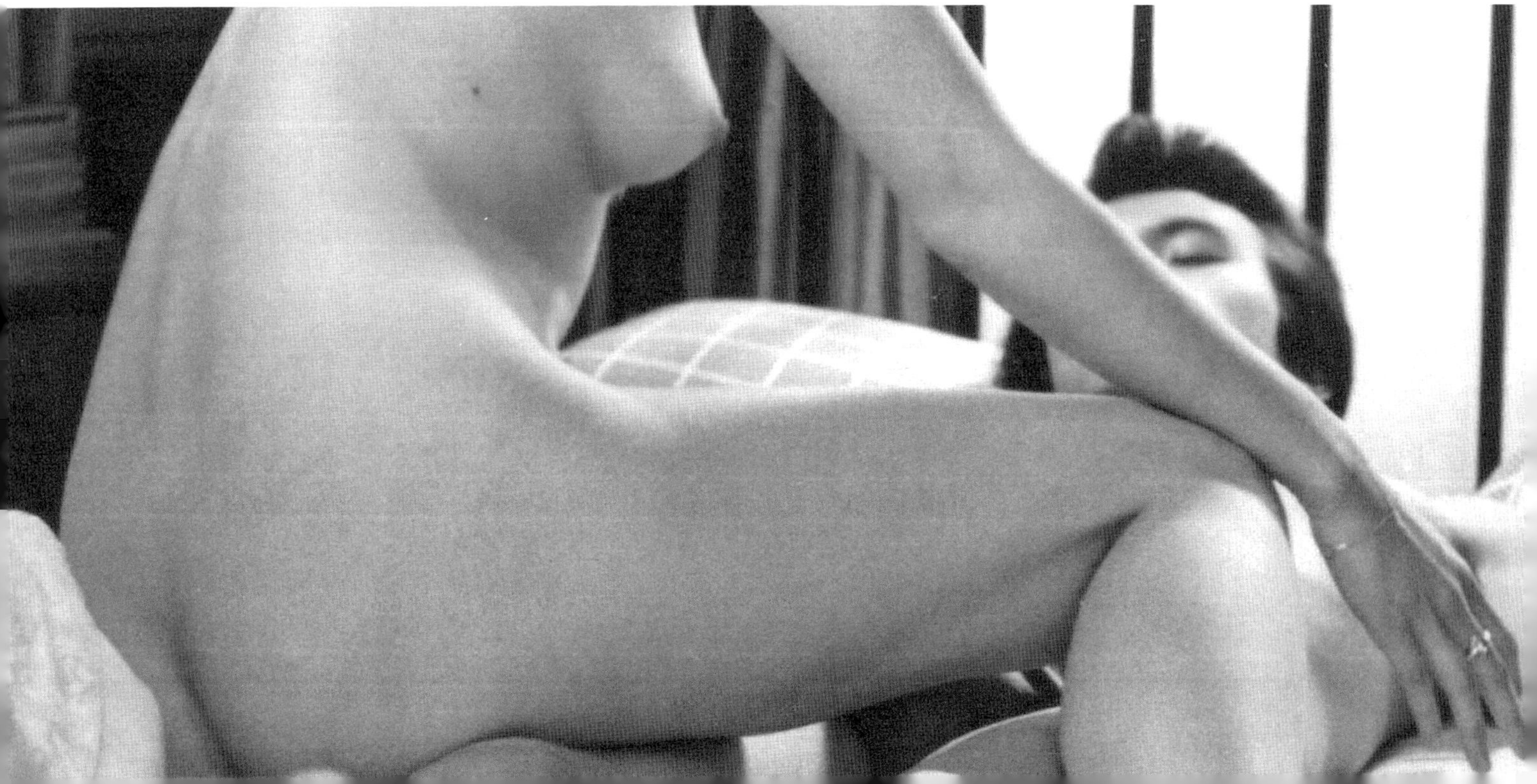

淫乱な指 [映倫]

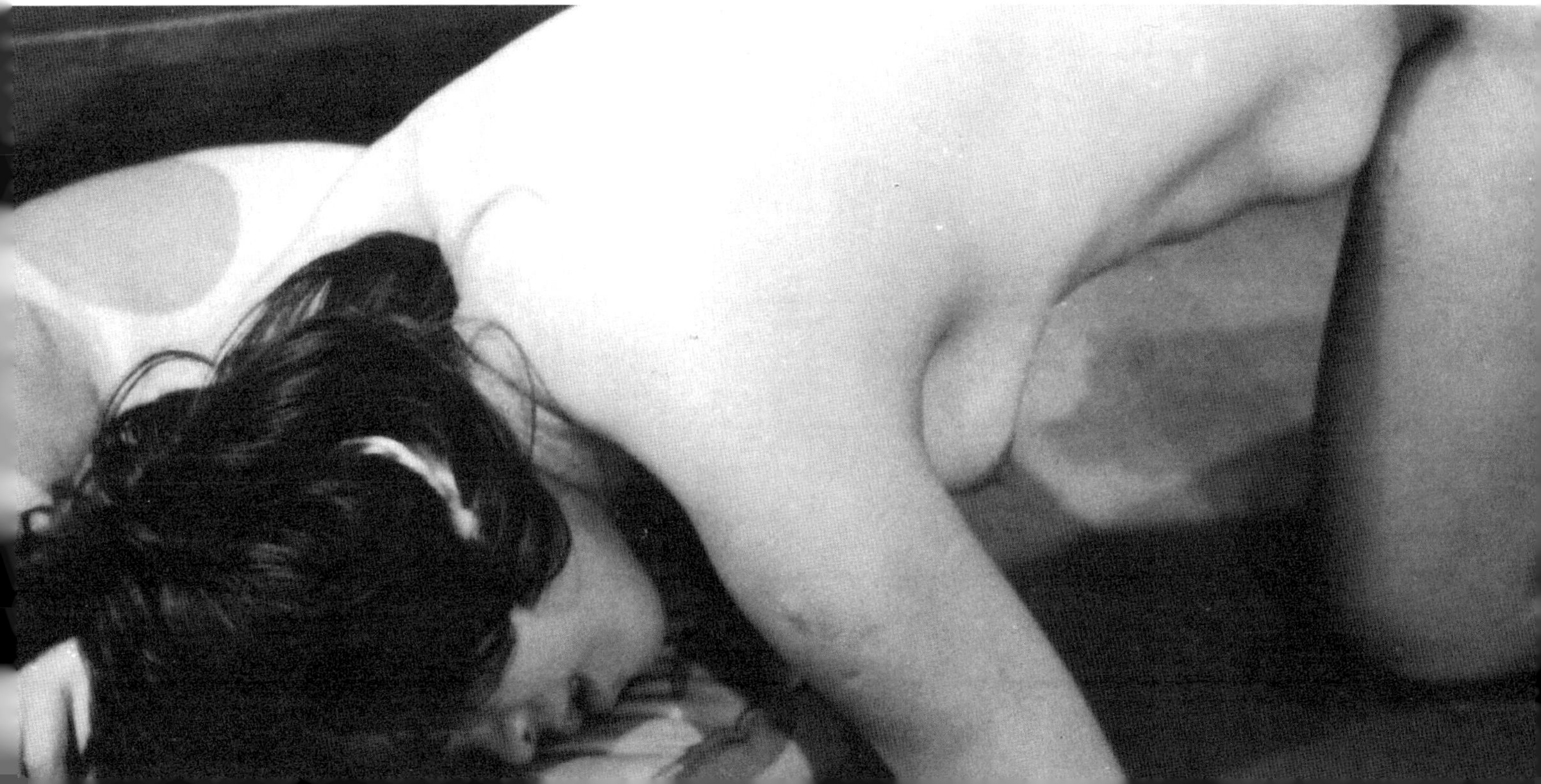

女子大生 ザ・穴場

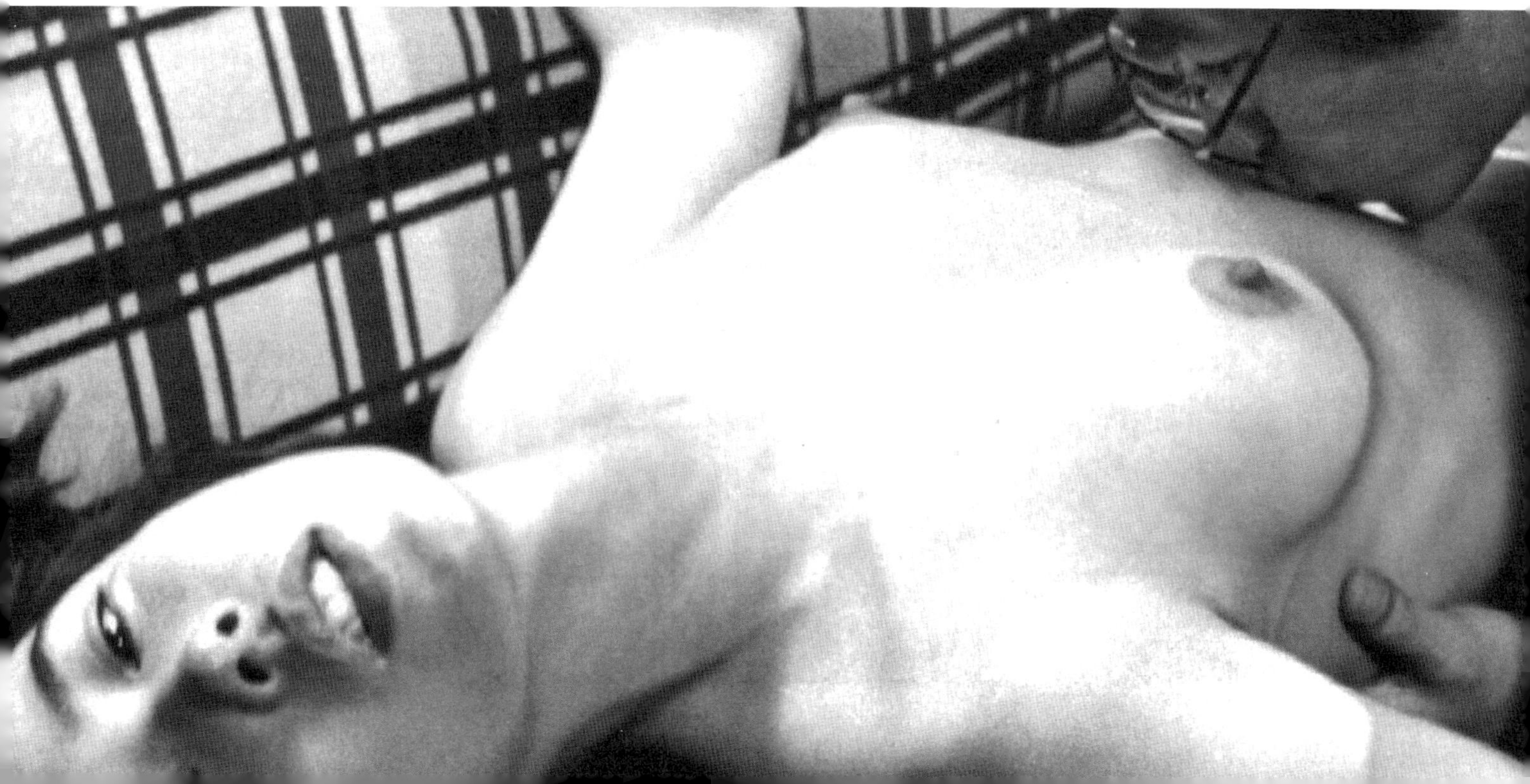

下半身美人 狂いそう

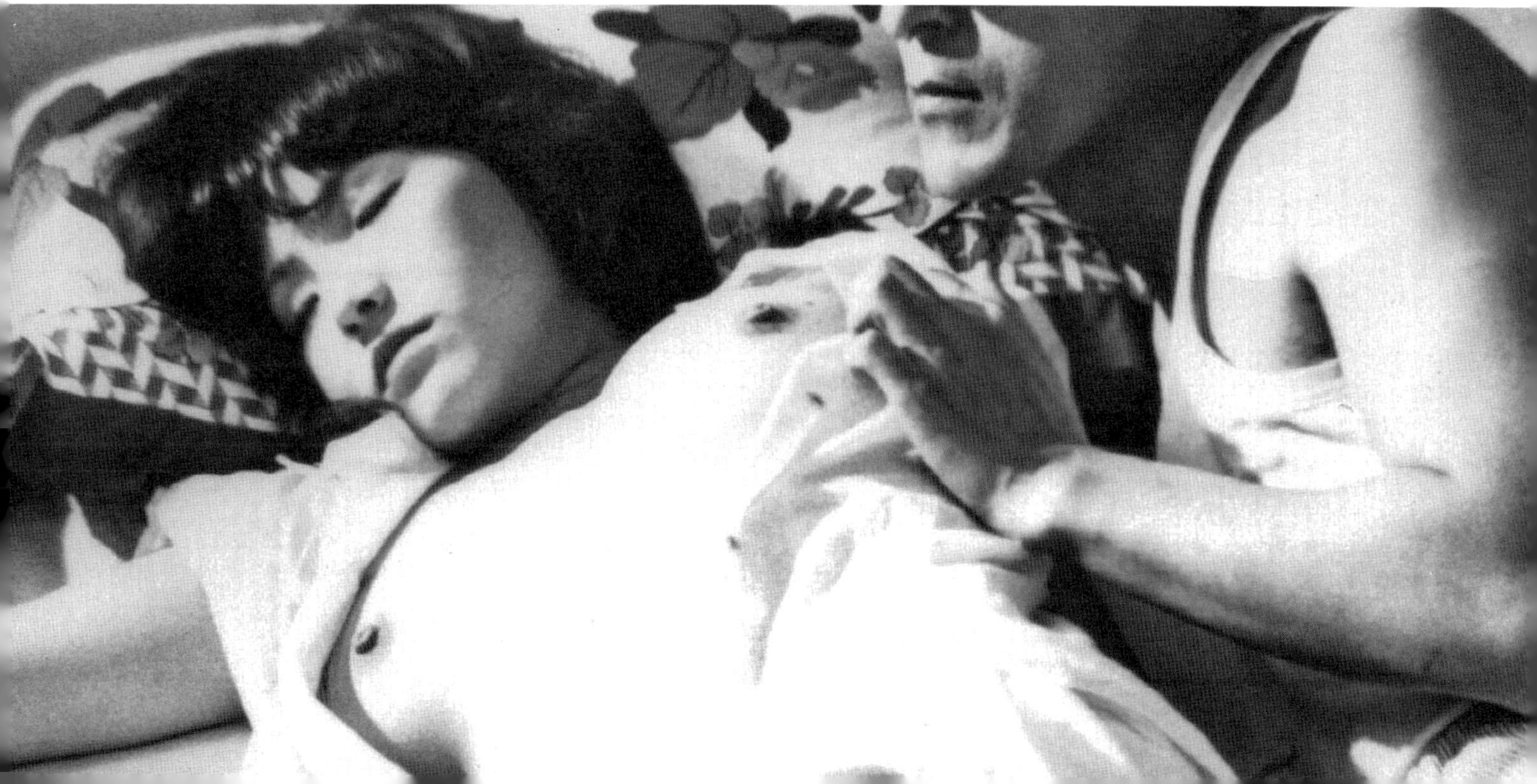

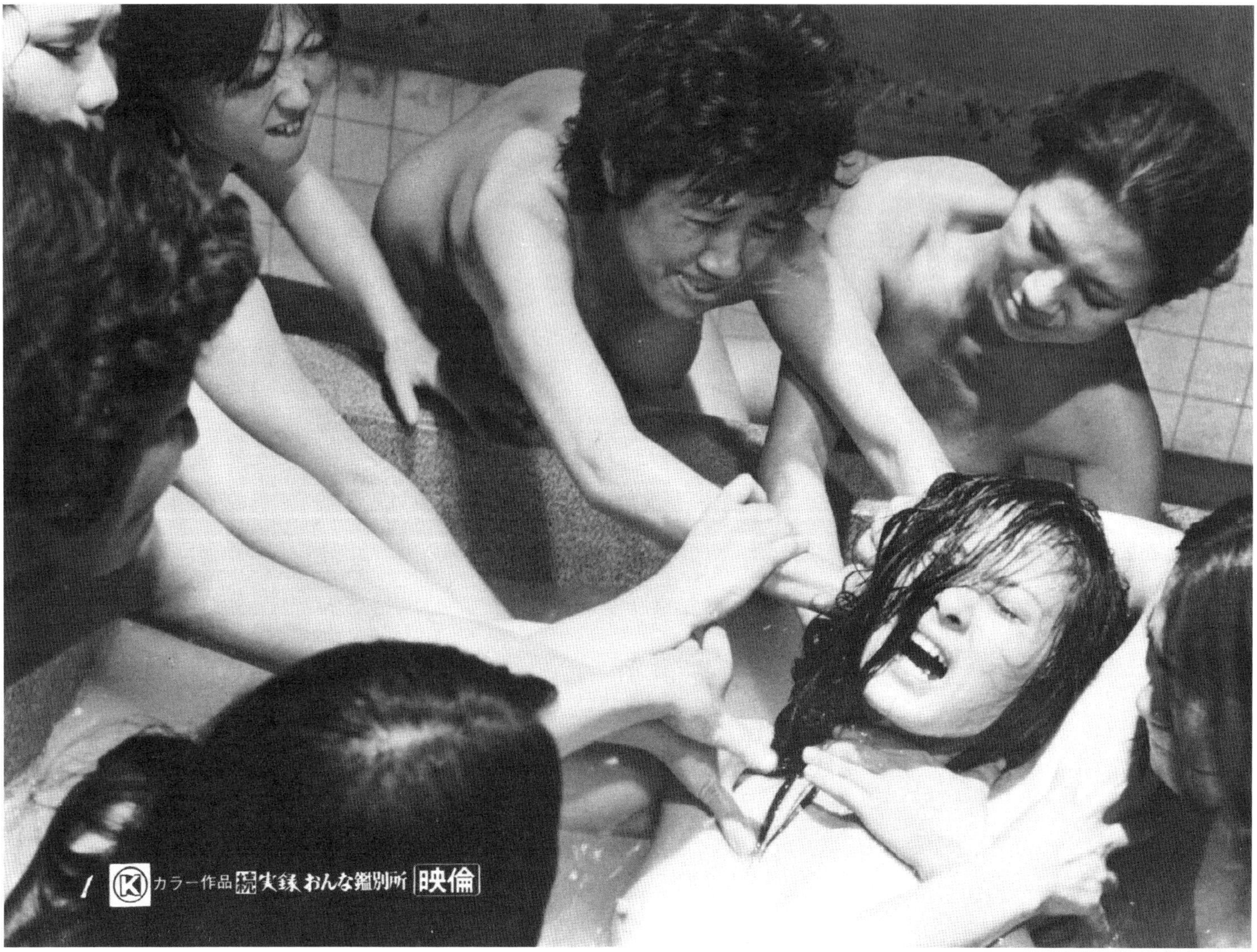

カラー作品 続実録 おんな鑑別所 映倫

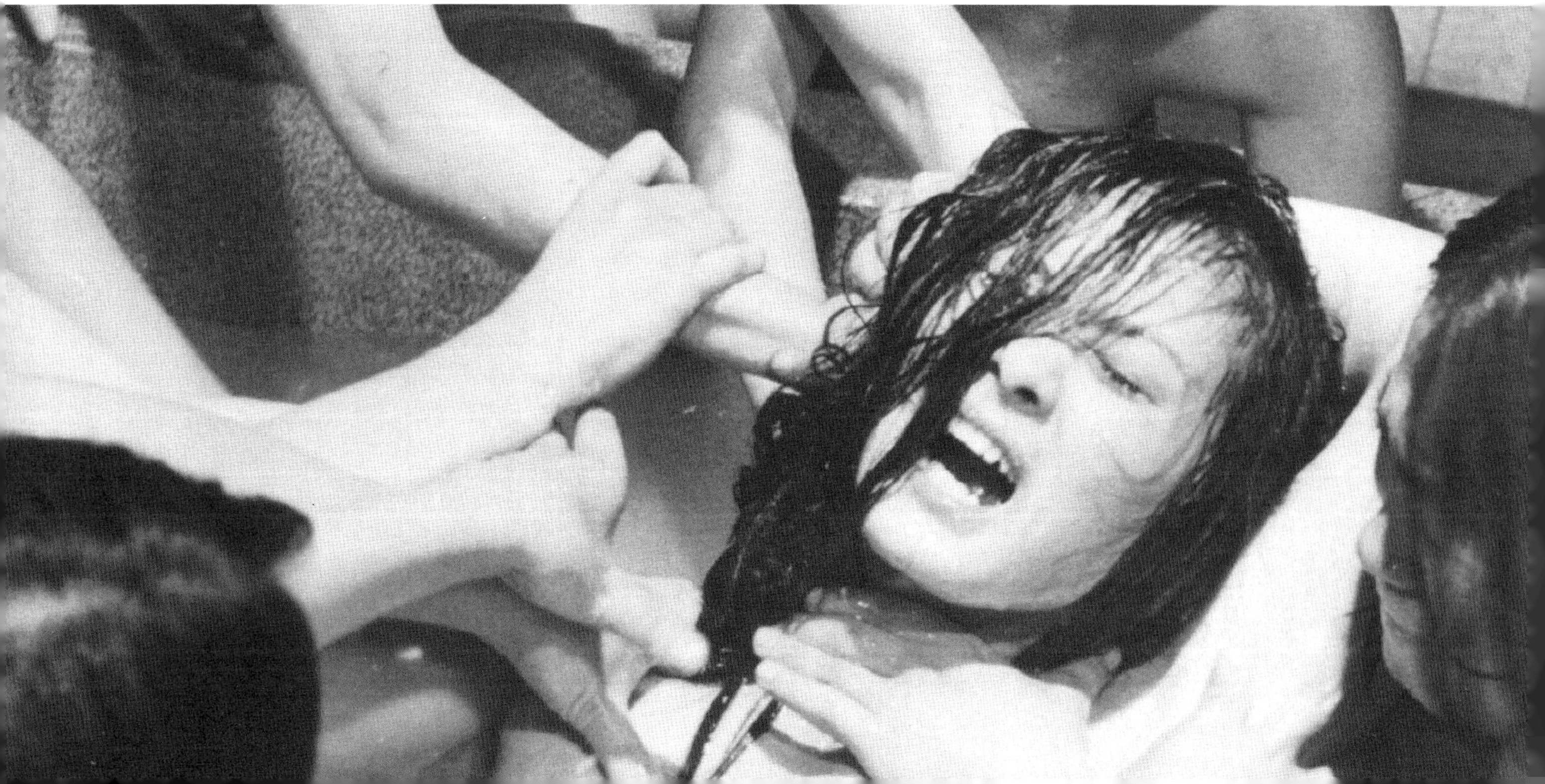

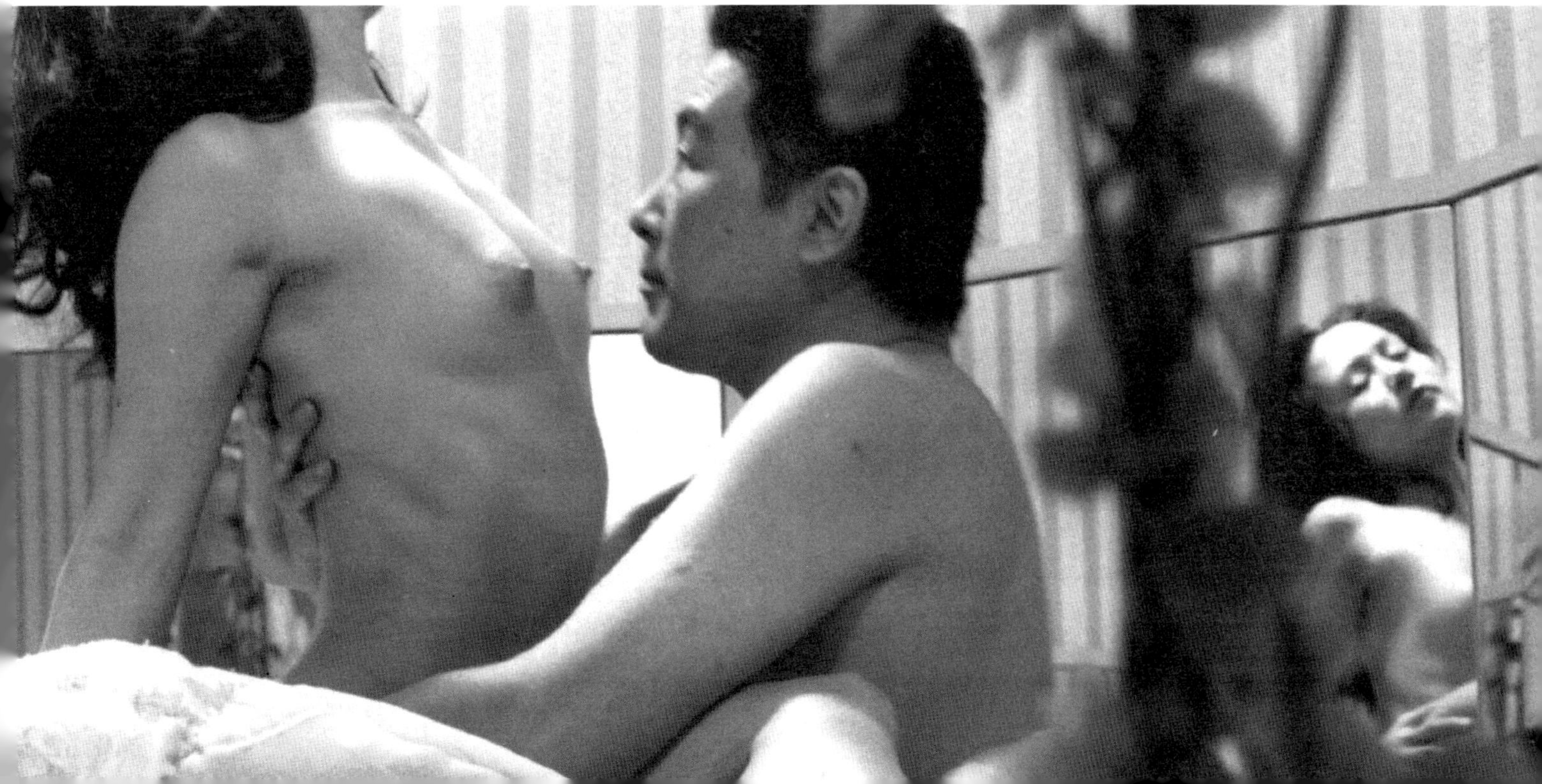

オールカラー 白い天使の抱擁 映倫2

痴漢のideo 映像

オールカラー 変身

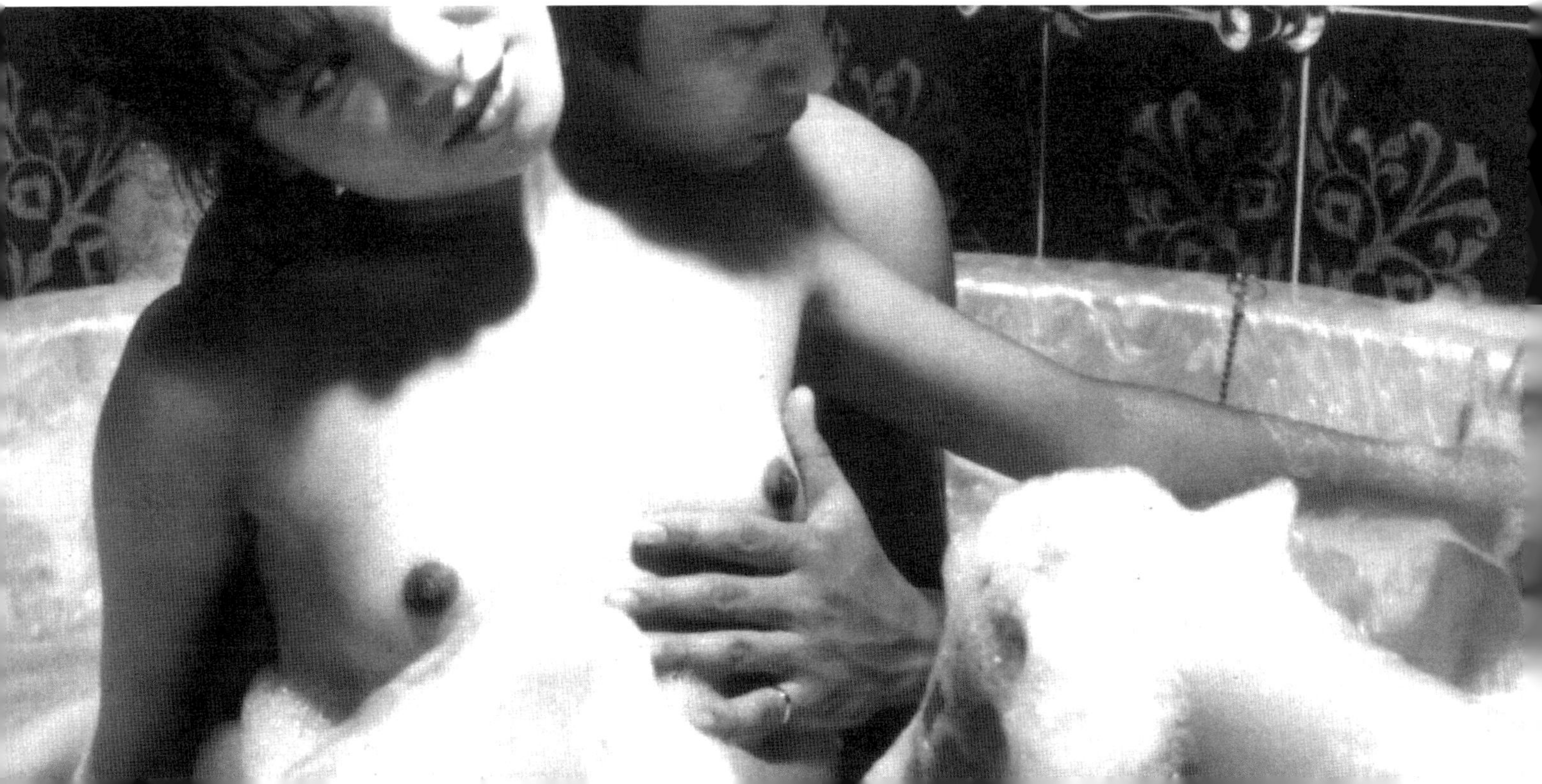

暴行三人組 |映倫|

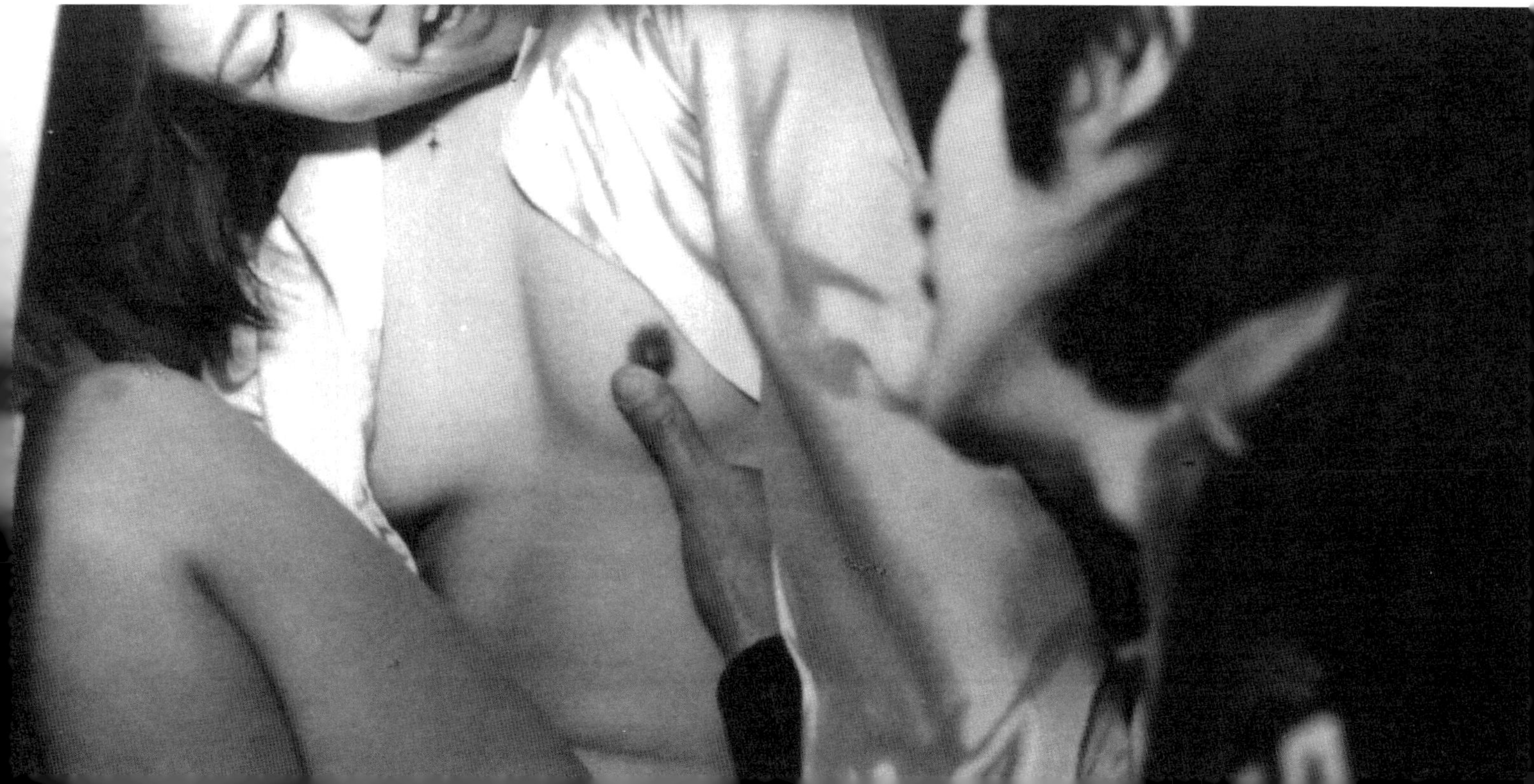

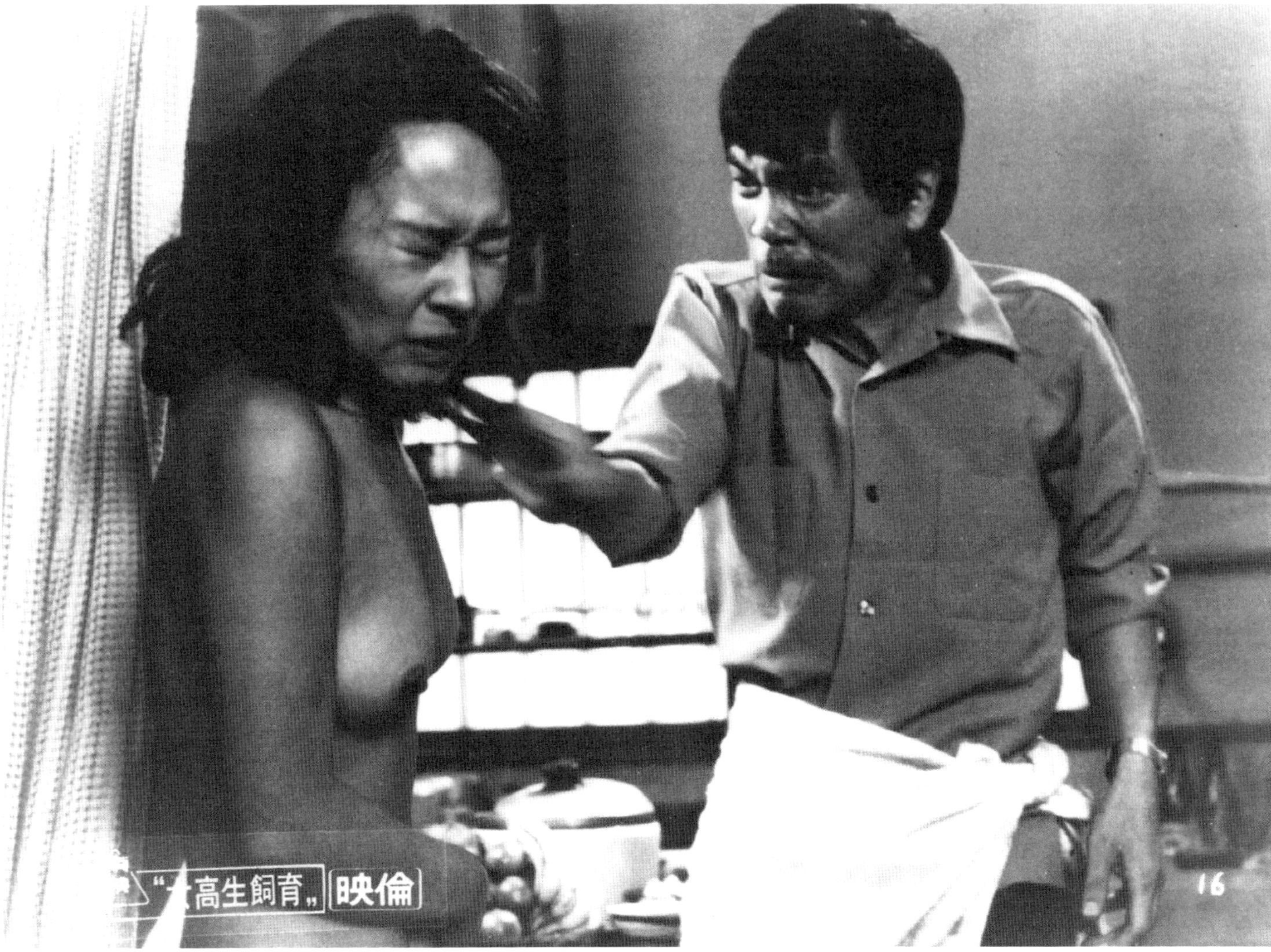

"女高生飼育" 映倫

16

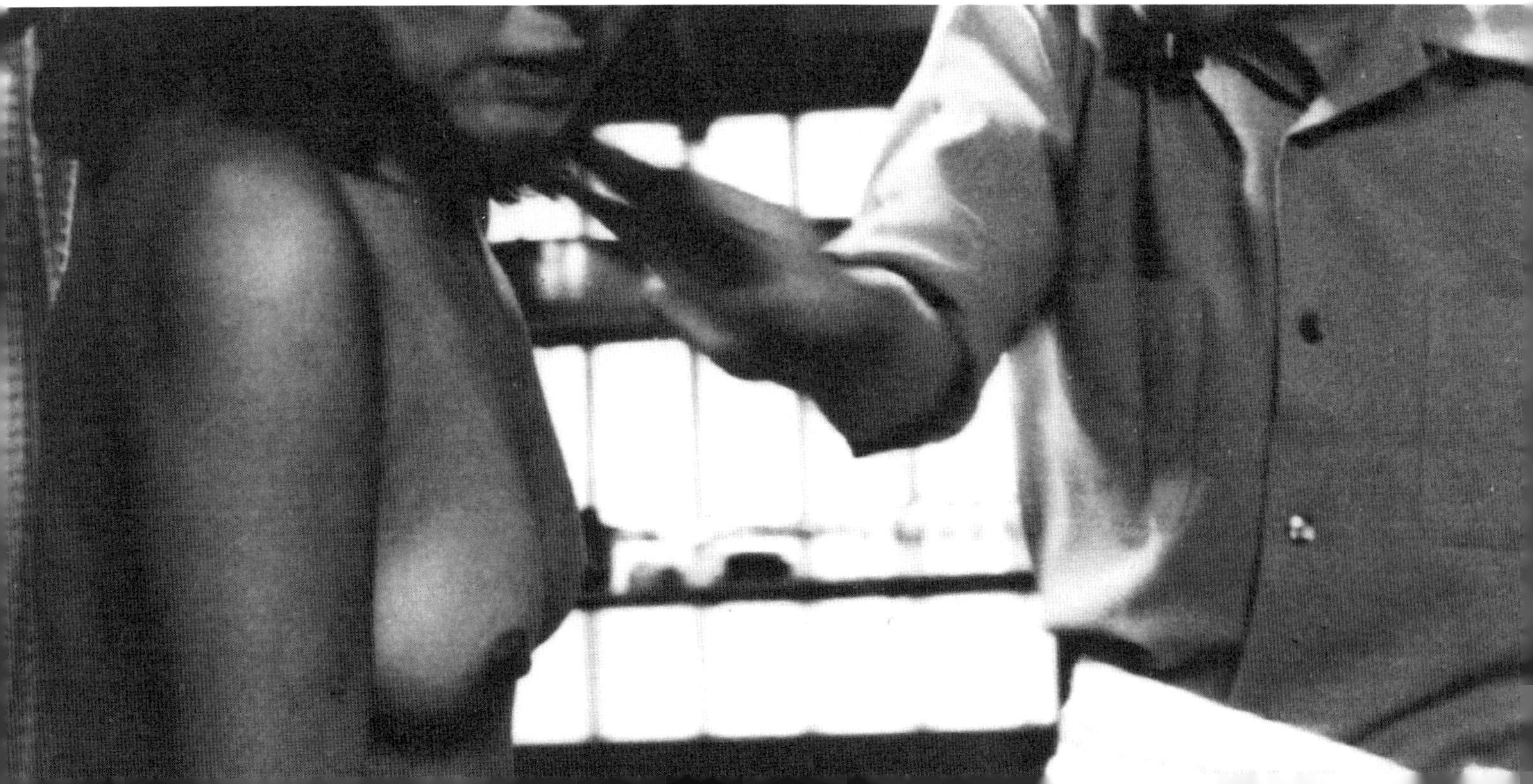

23 カラー作品
蜘蛛の湯女

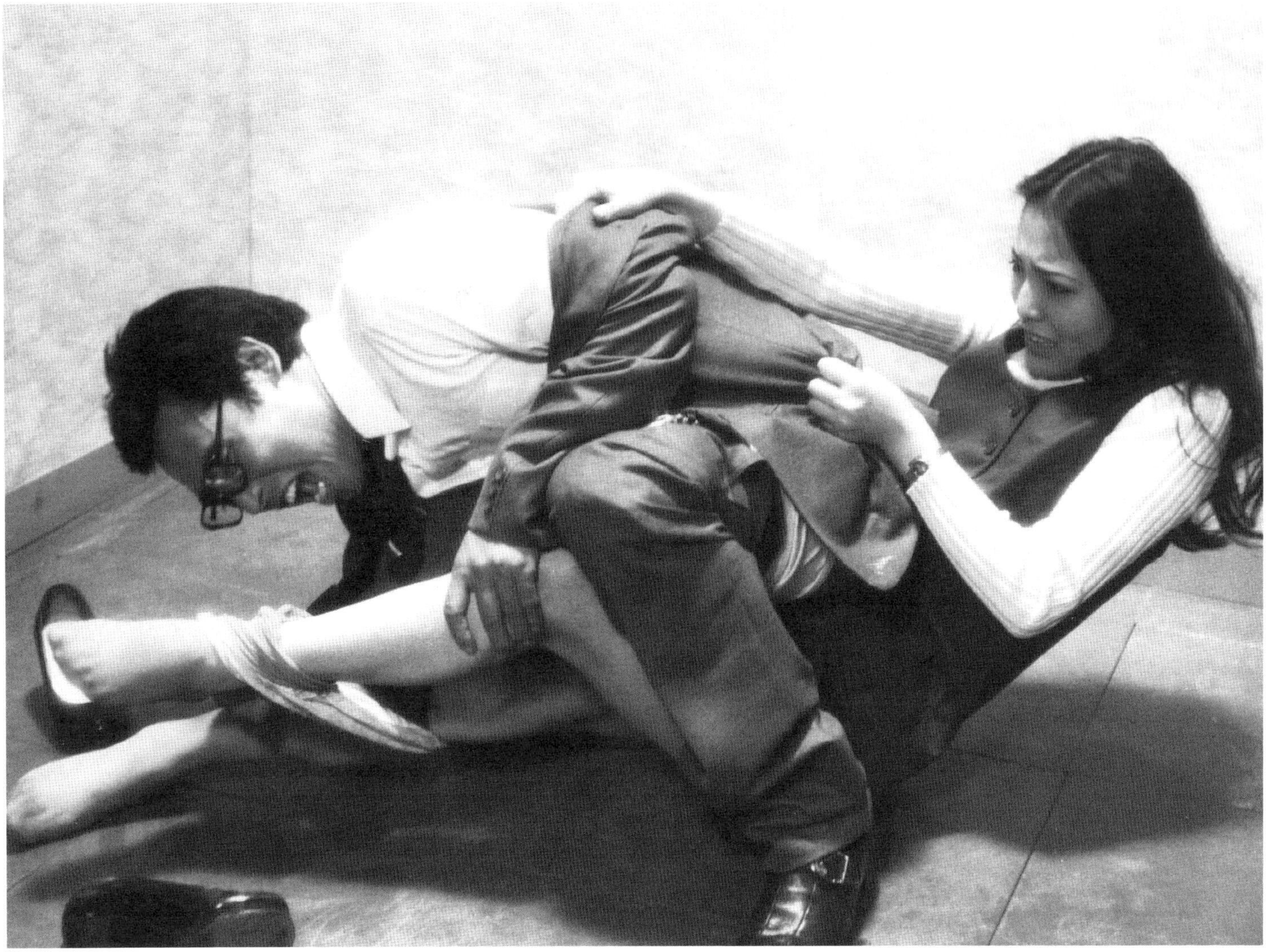

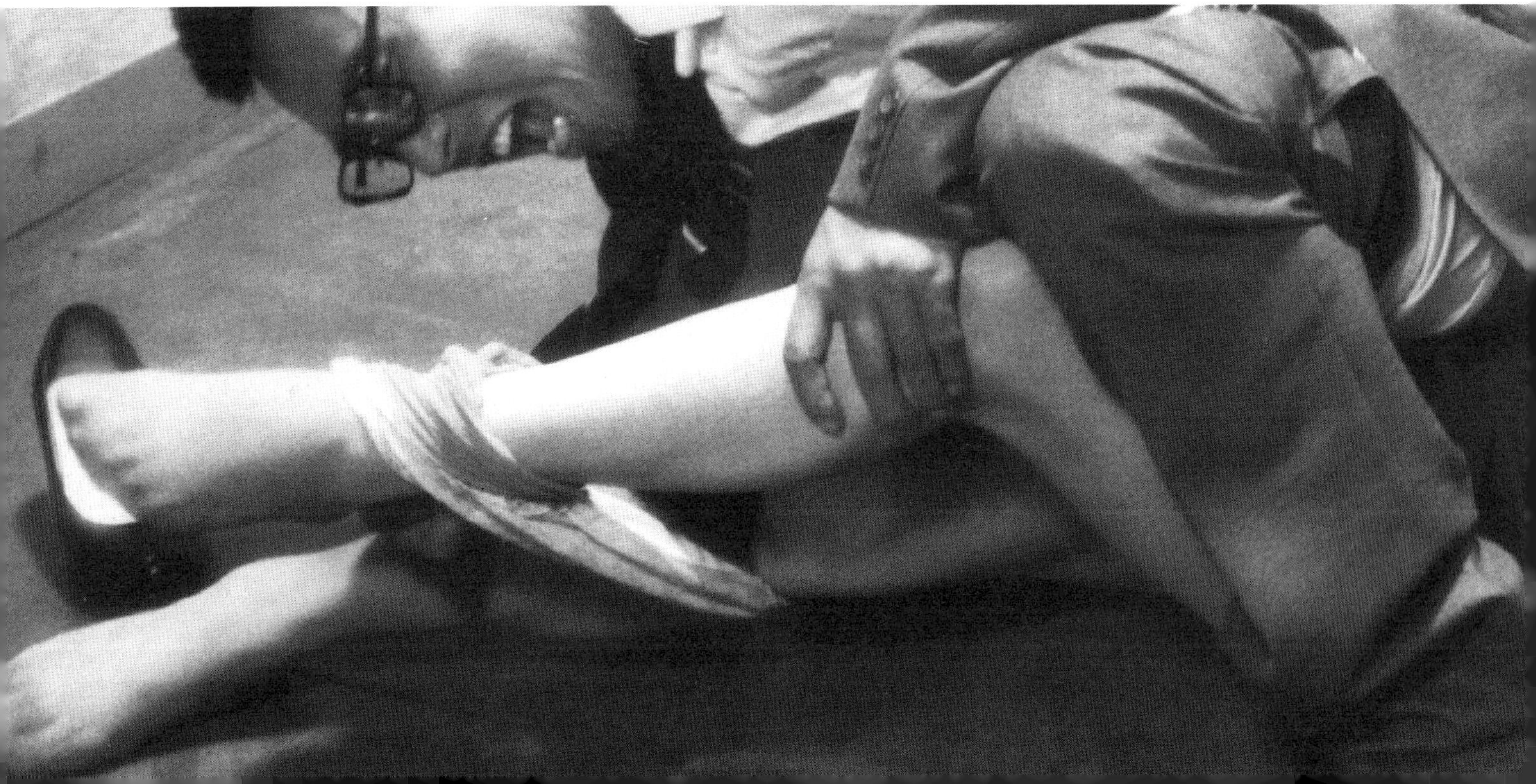

映倫 セックス

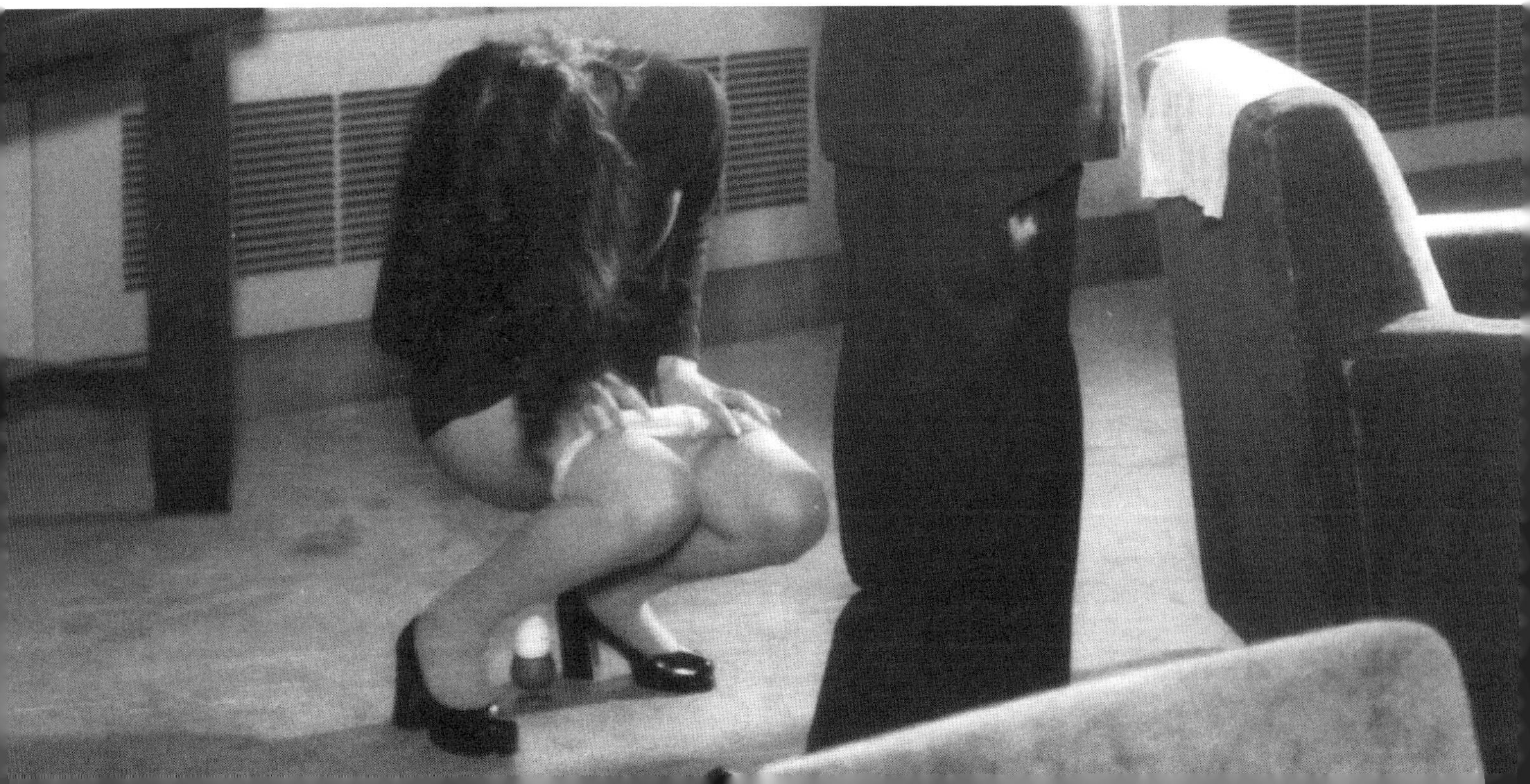

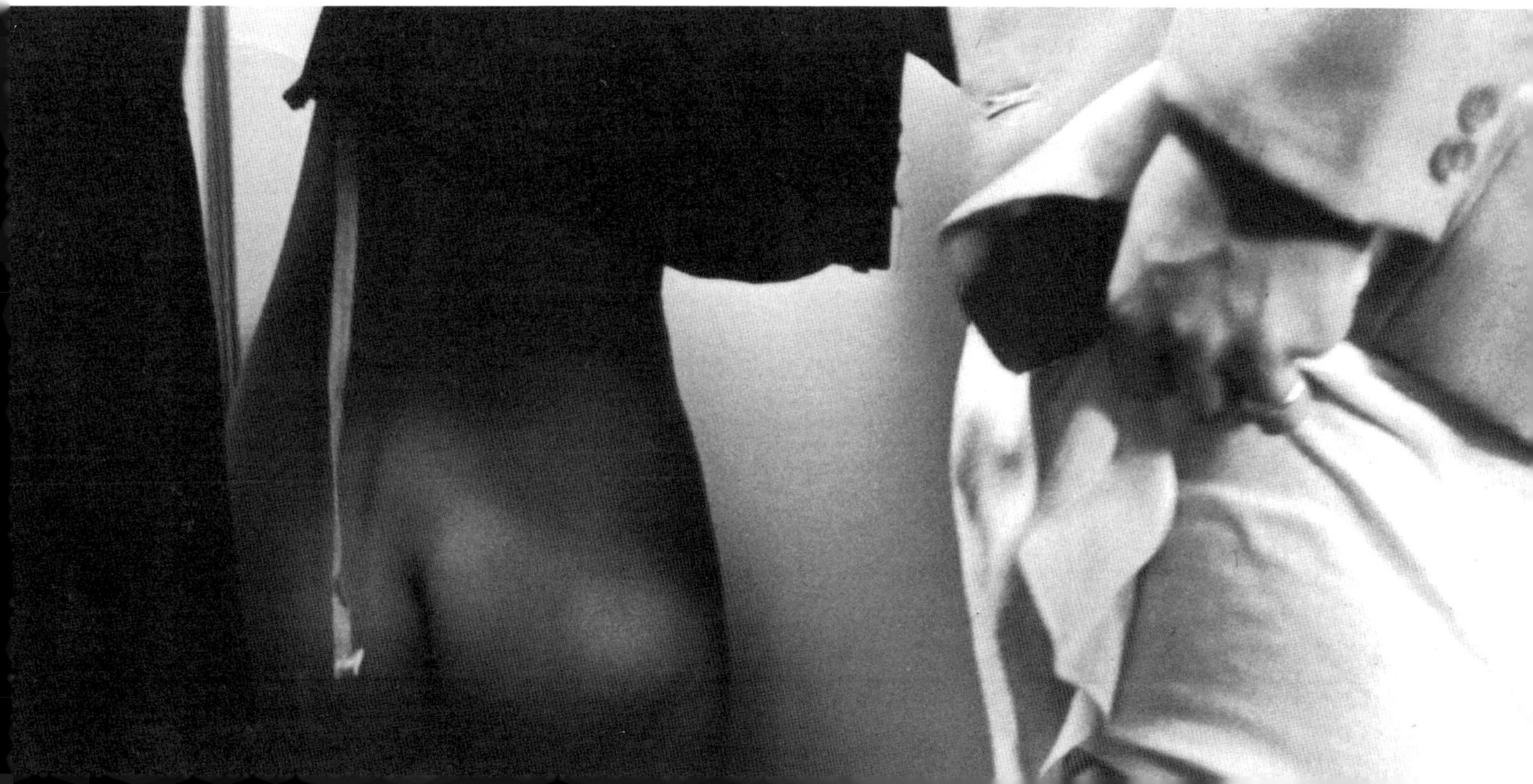

カラー作品
姉妹の湯女

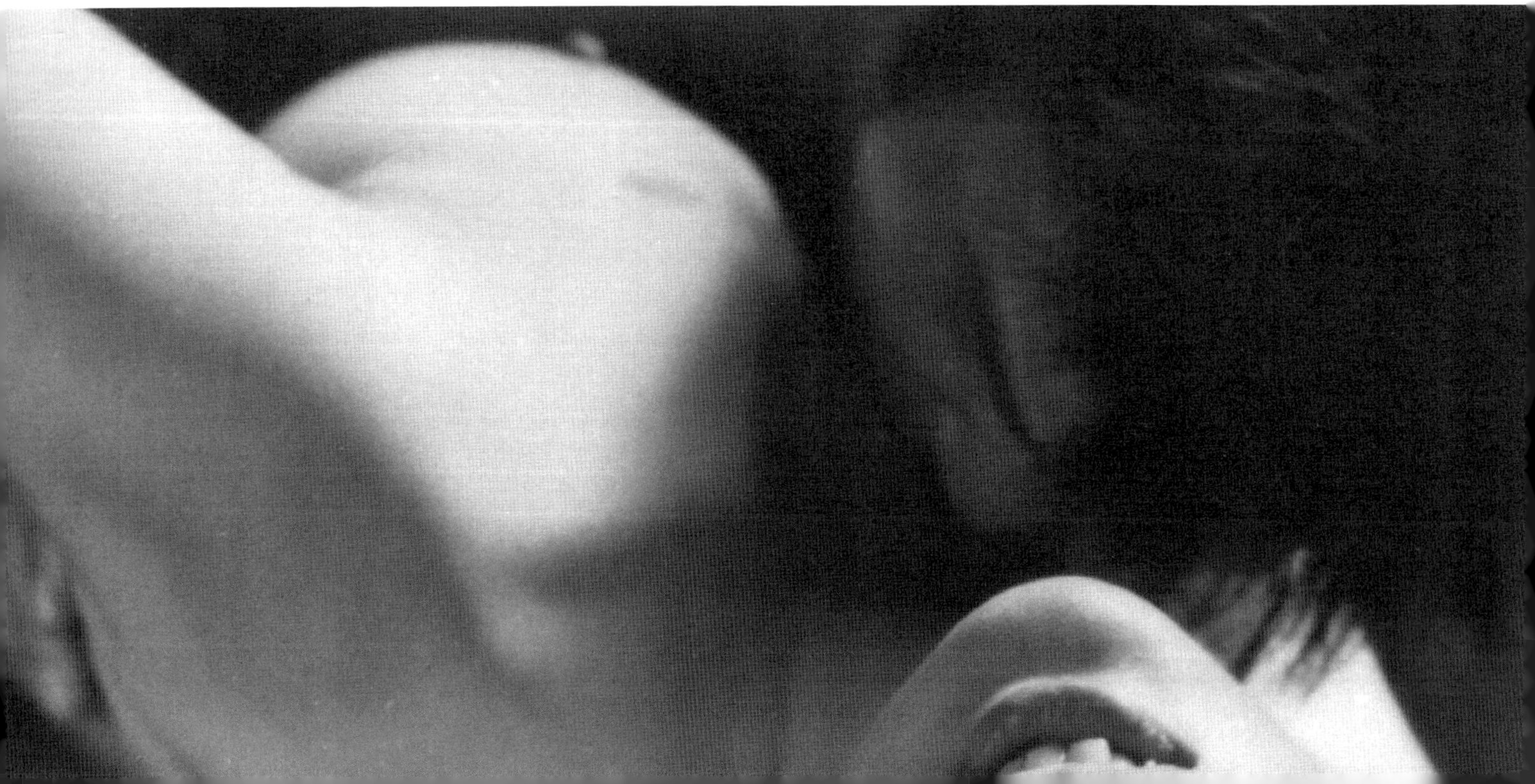

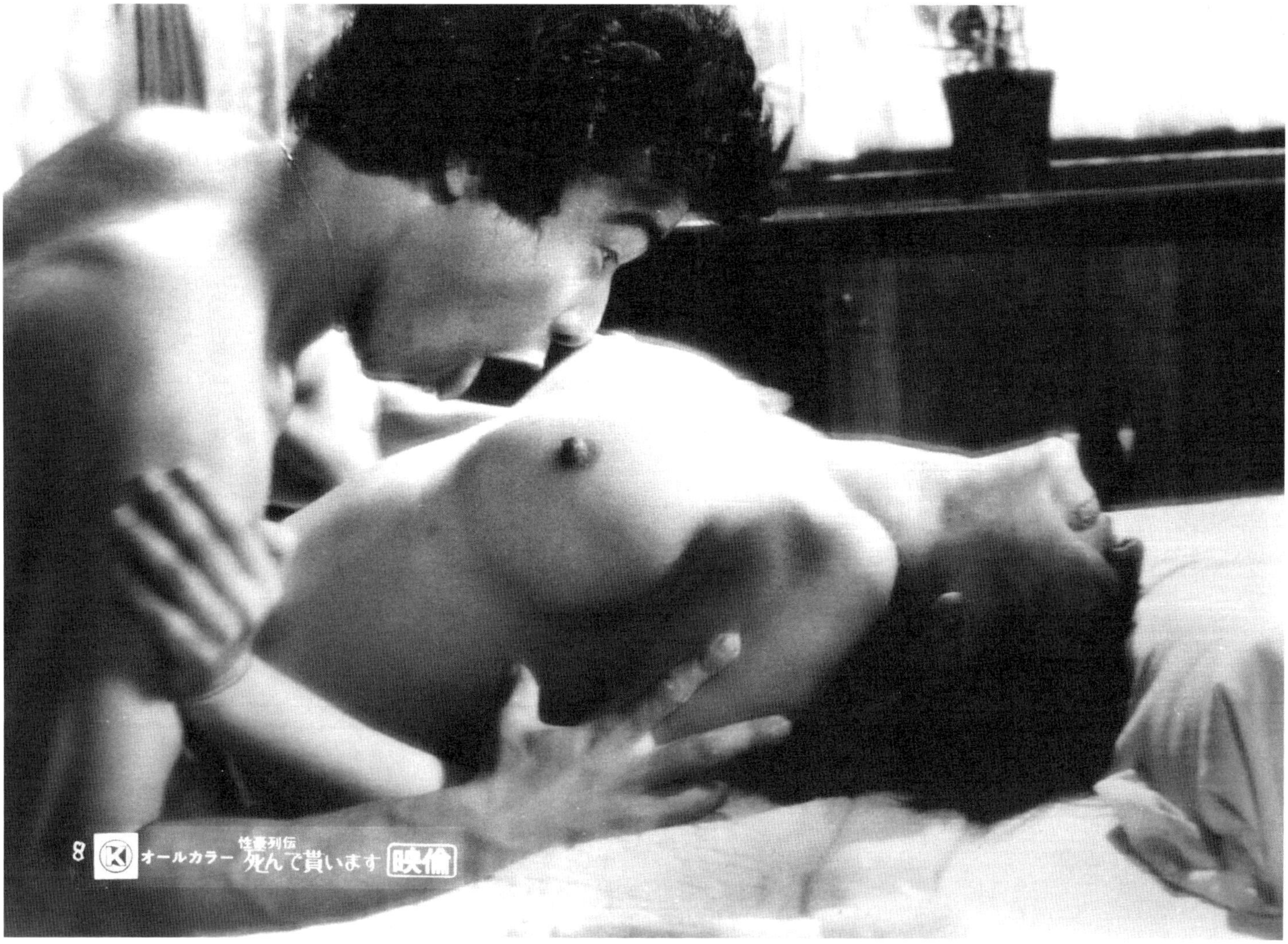

8 オールカラー 性豪列伝 死んで貰います 映倫

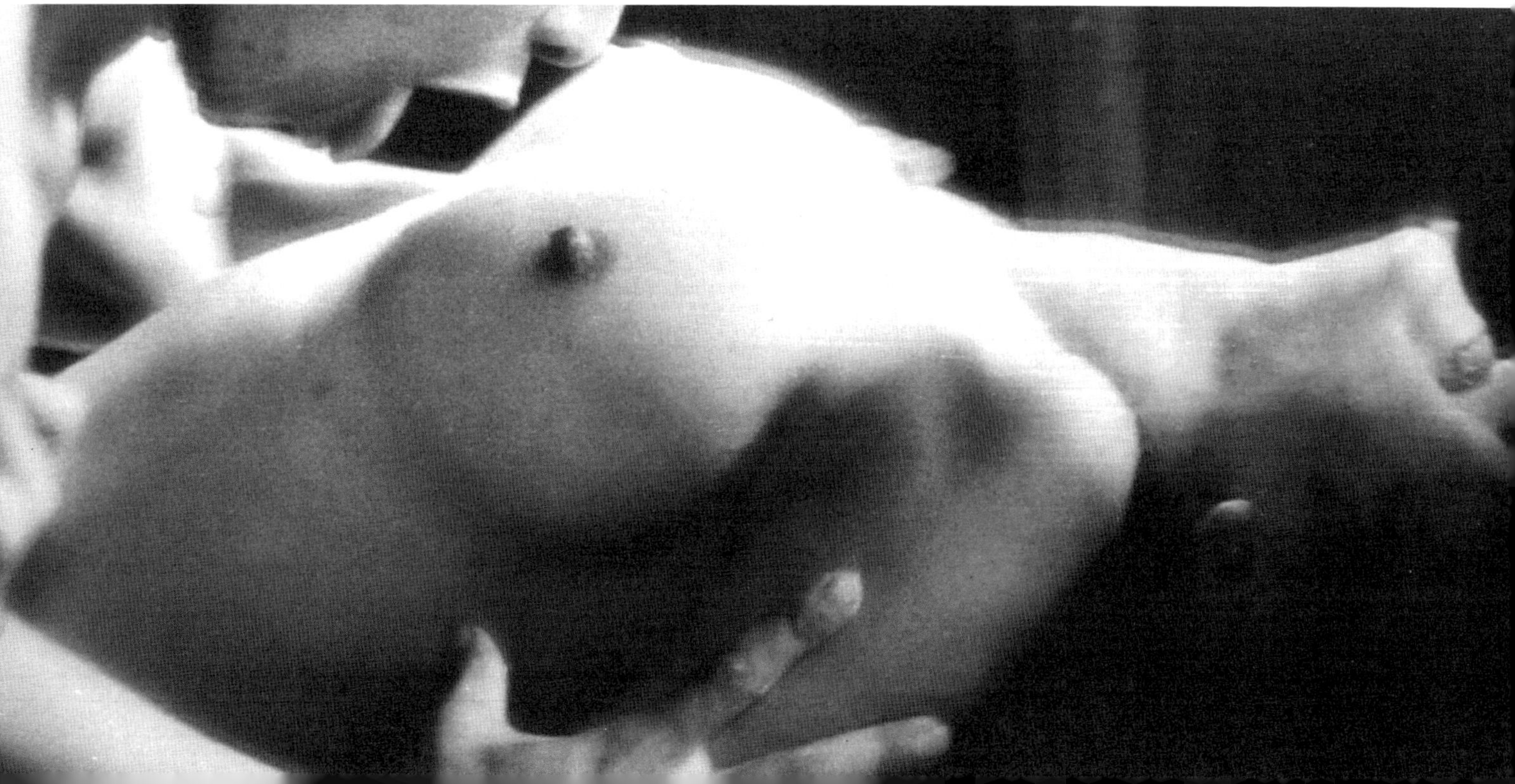

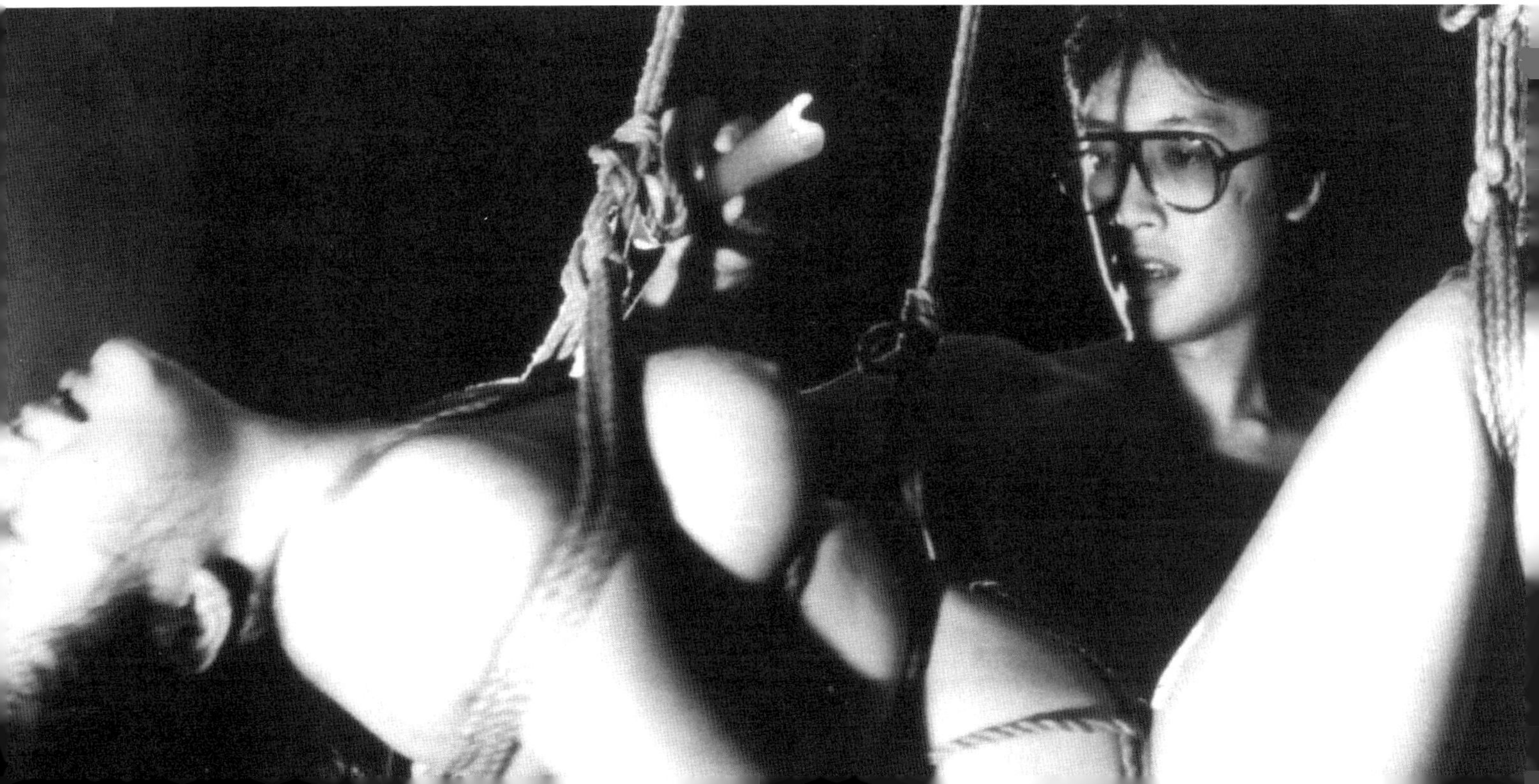

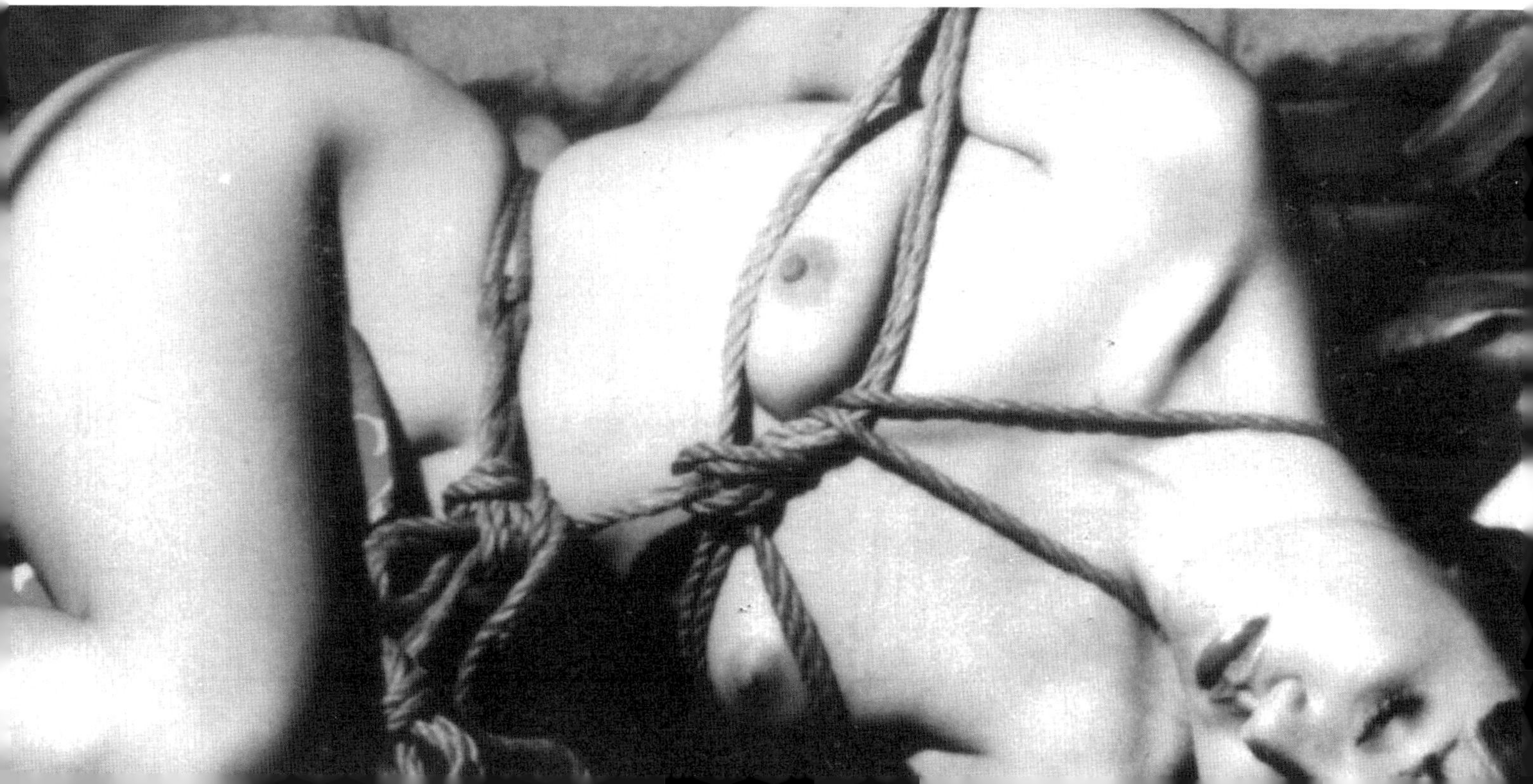

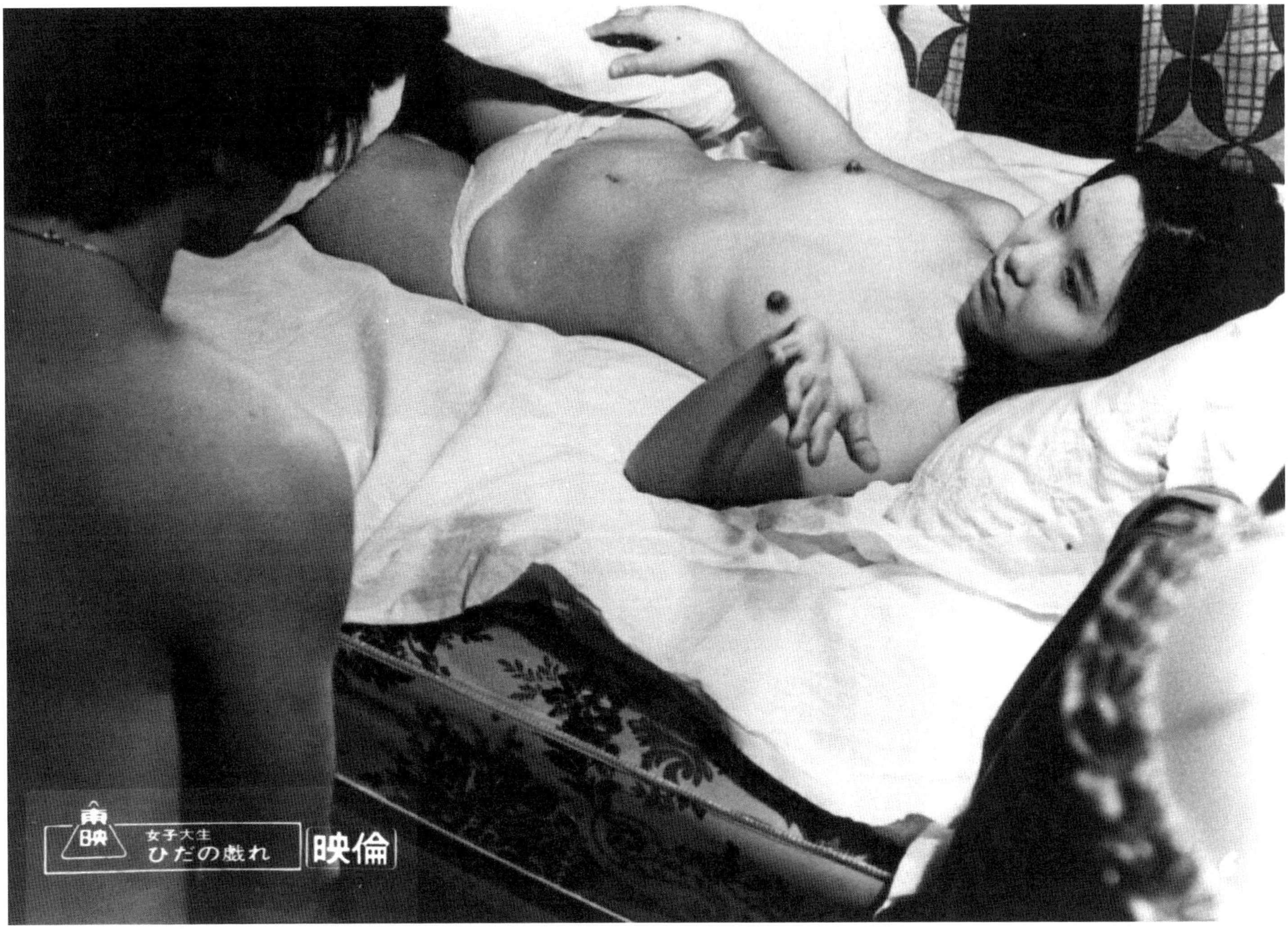

女子大生 ひだの戯れ 映倫

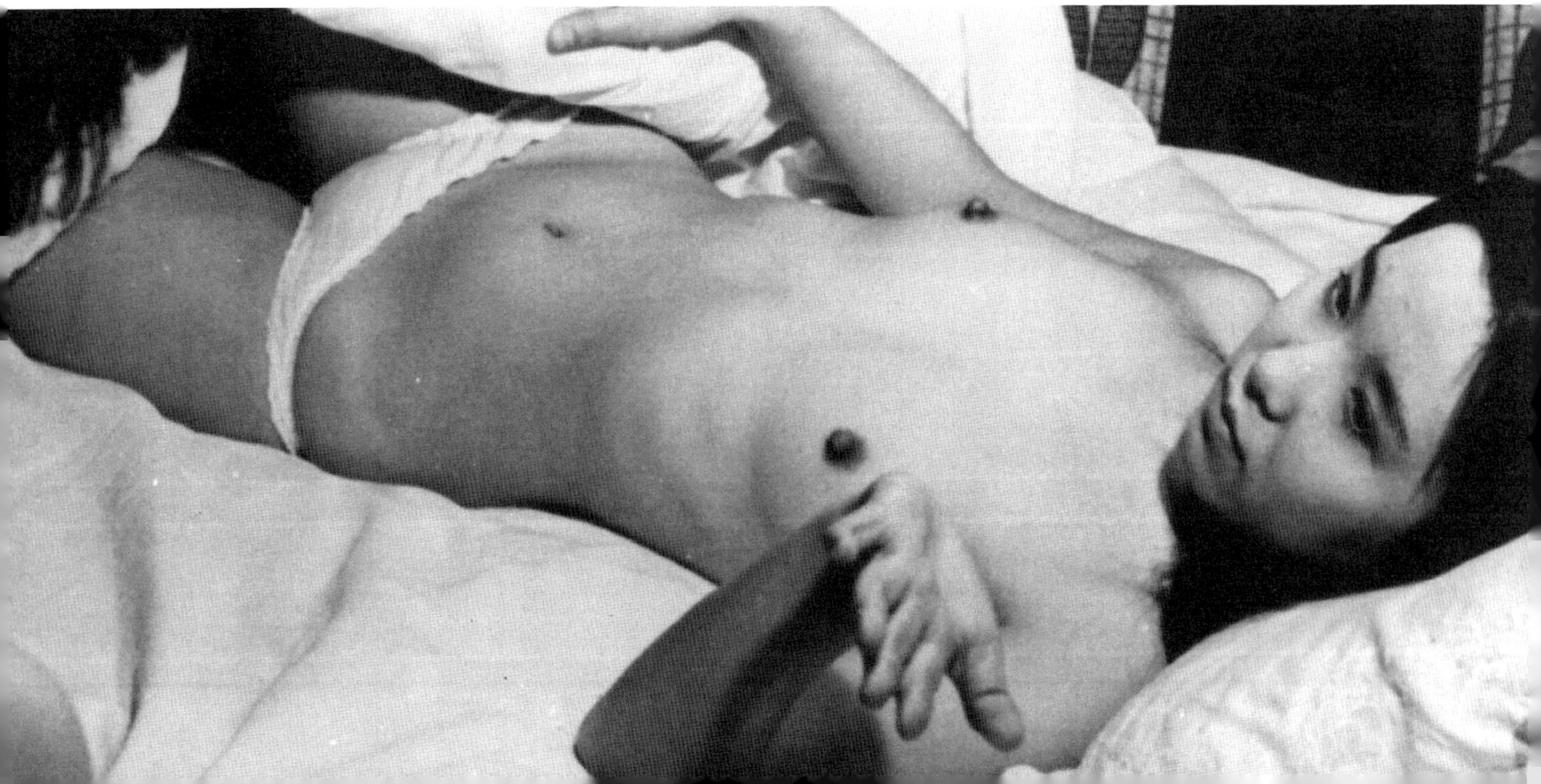

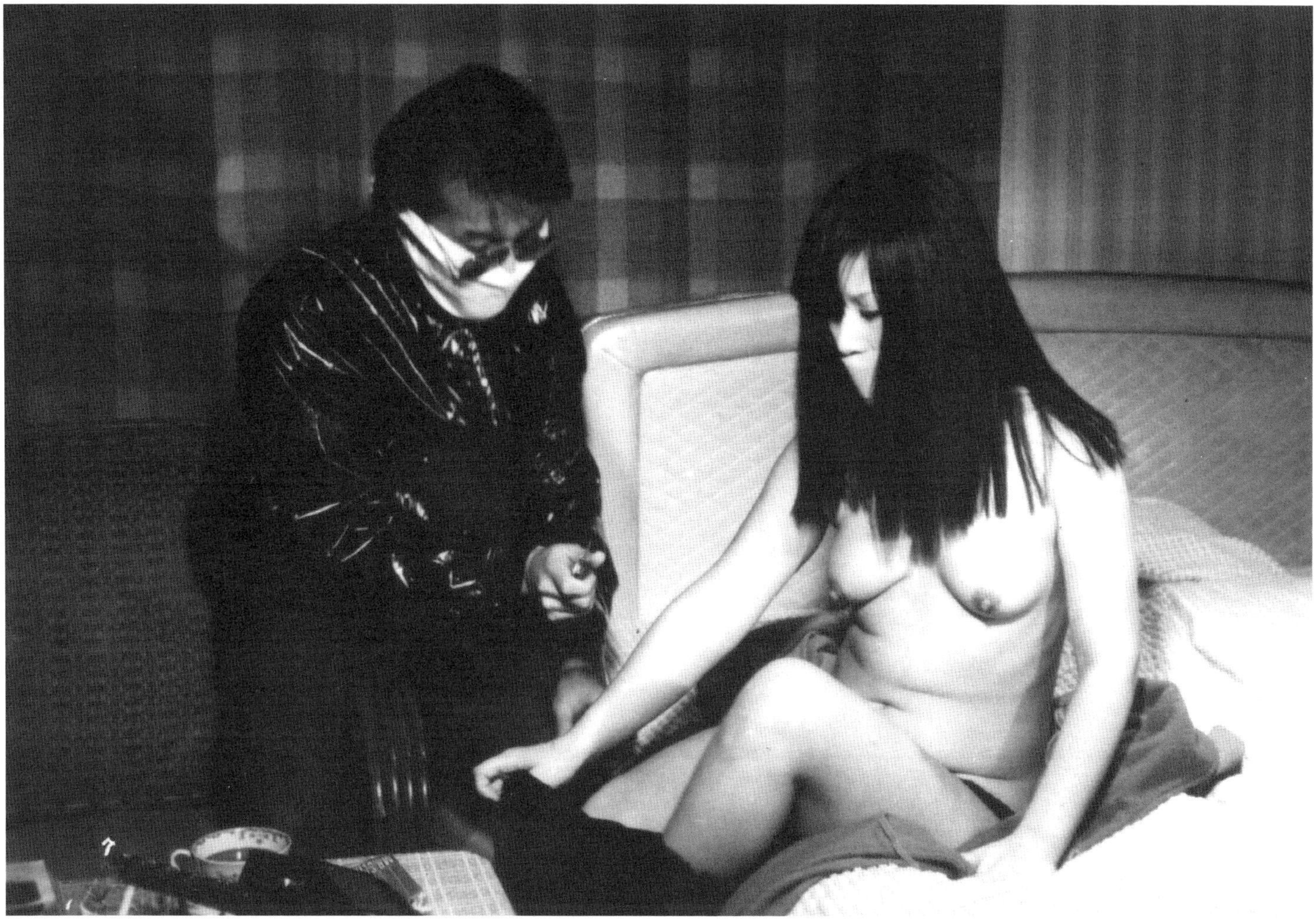

白い指の密戯 映倫

恐喝のテクニック
肉地獄

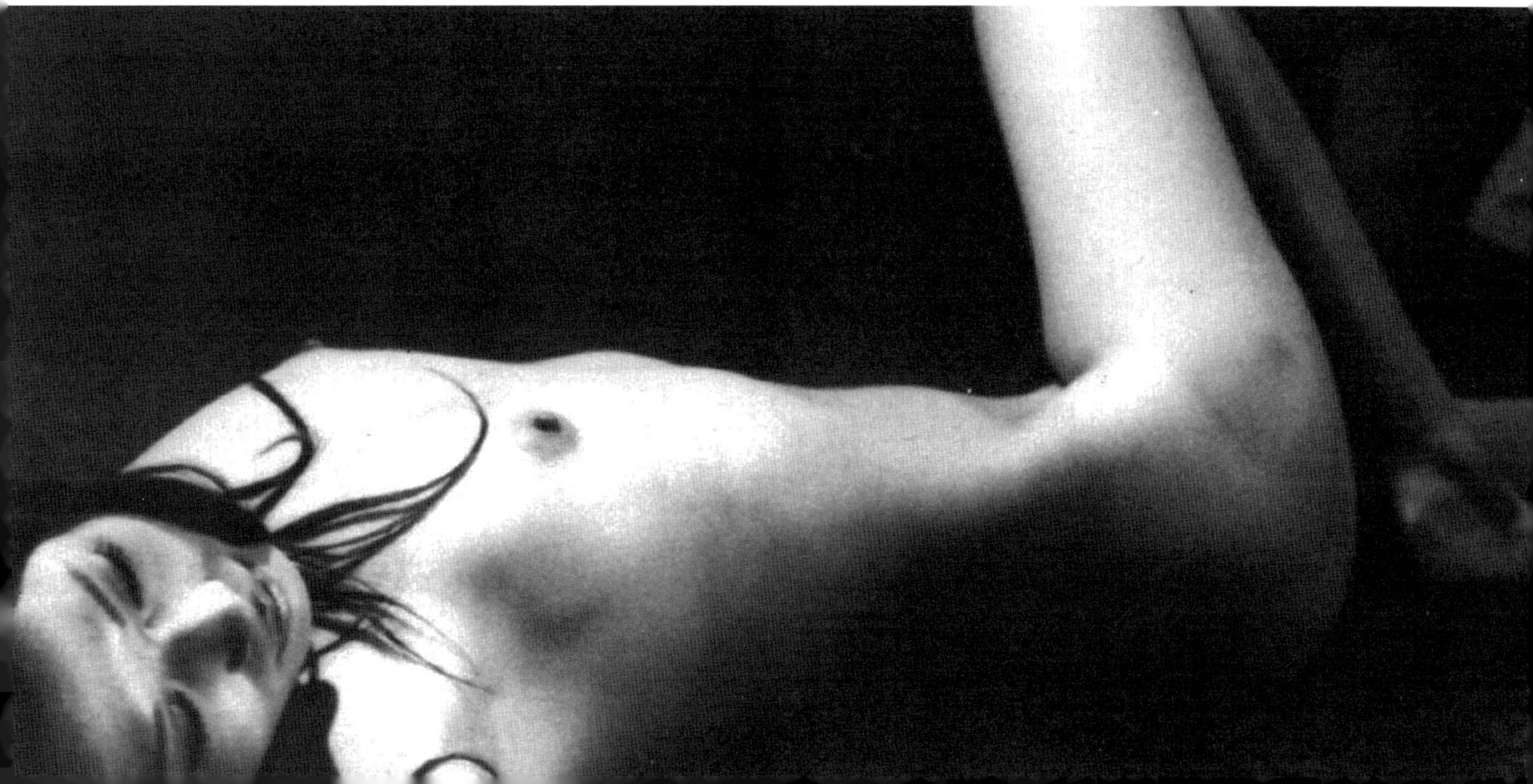

オールカラーお揉みいたします 映倫

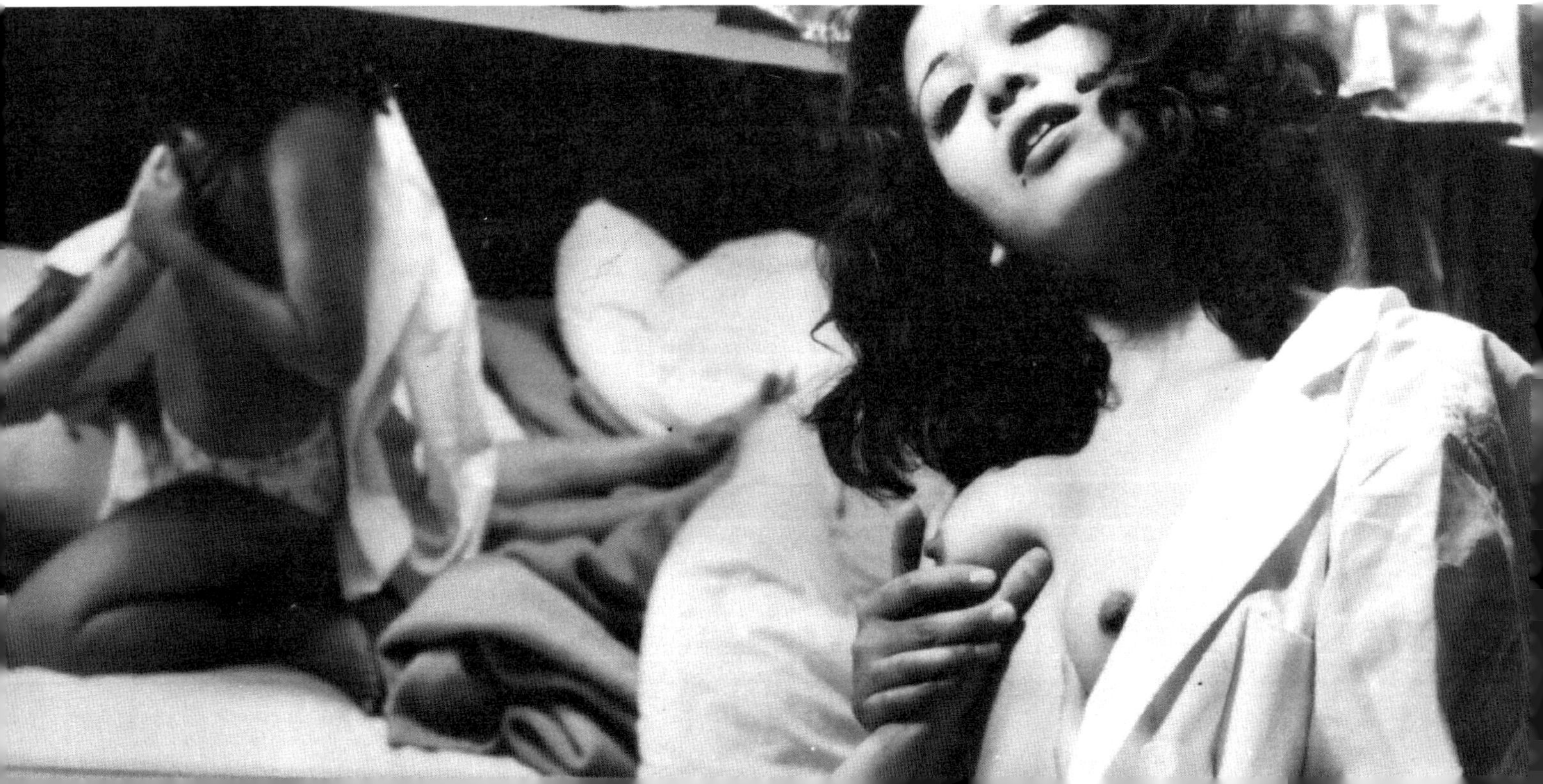

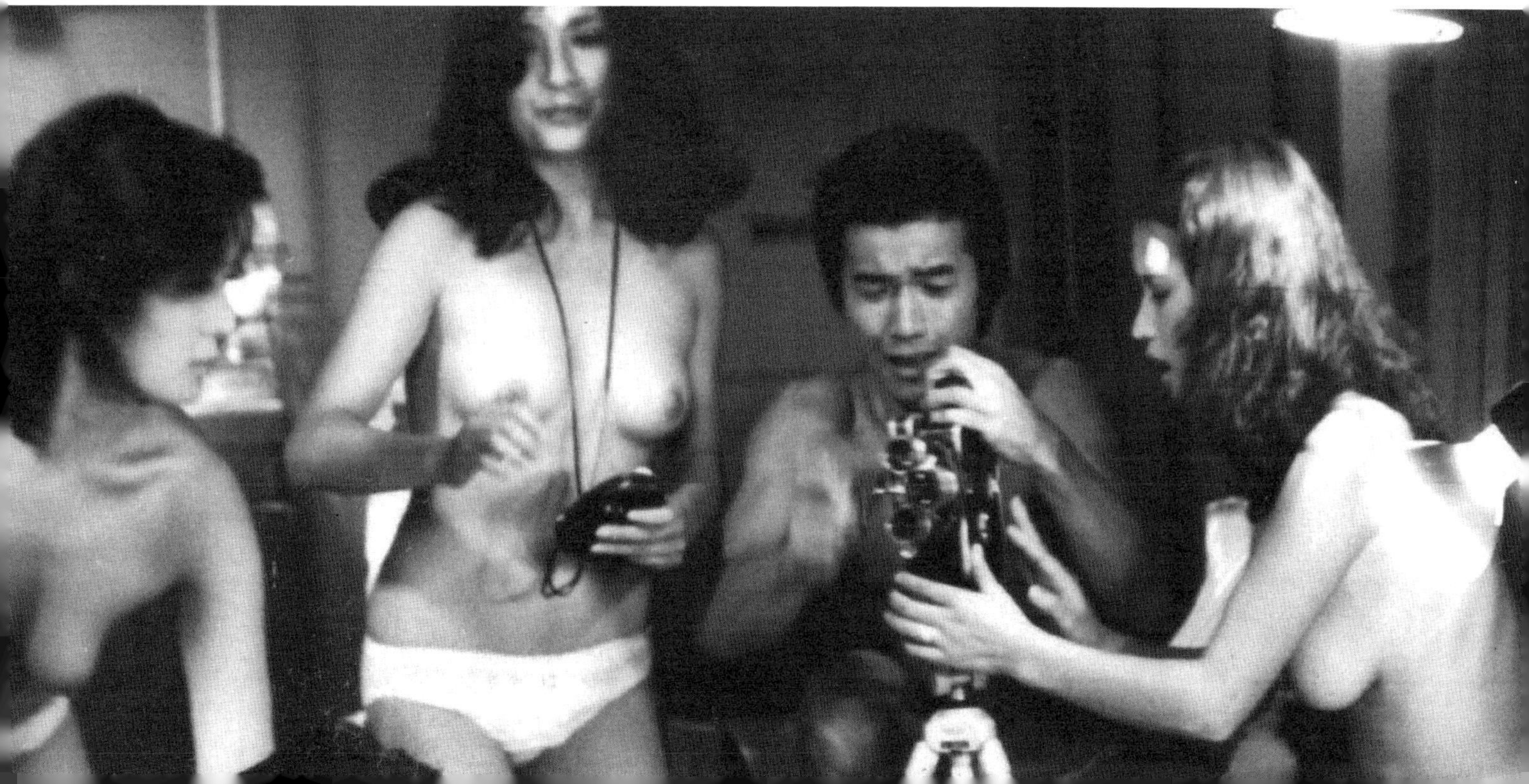

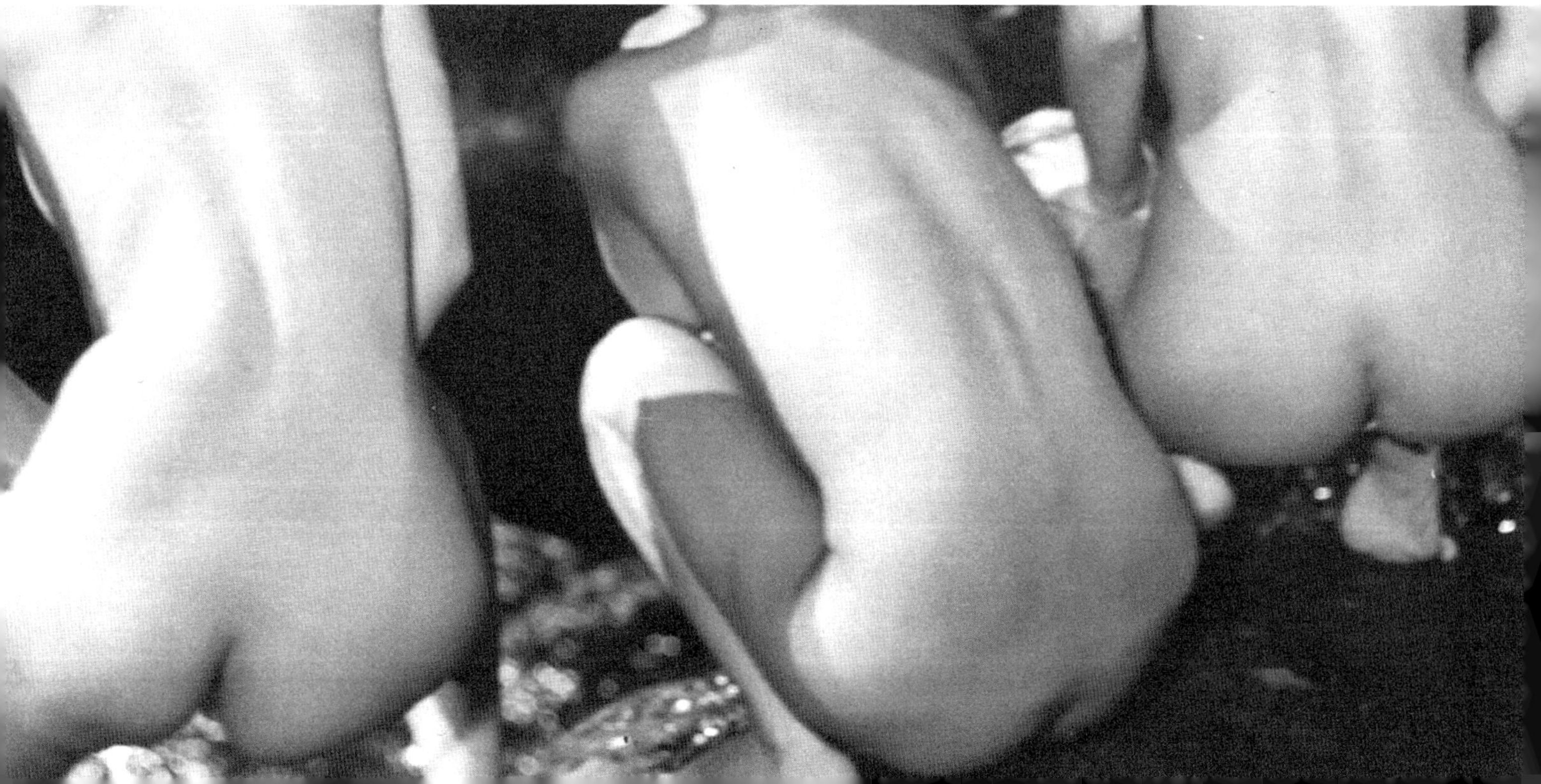

カラー作品 処女痴態 映倫 6 ★

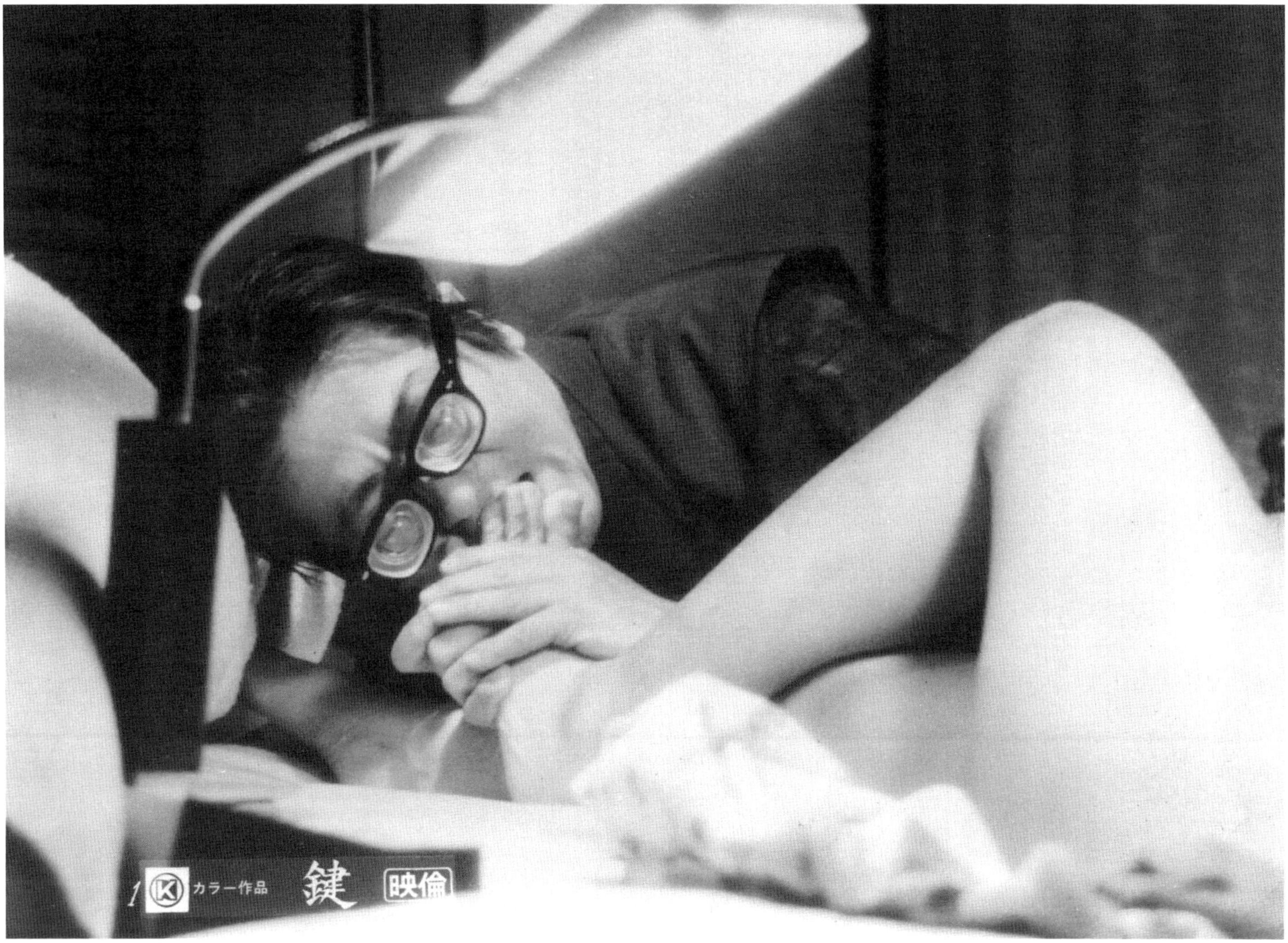

1 Ⓚ カラー作品 鍵 映倫

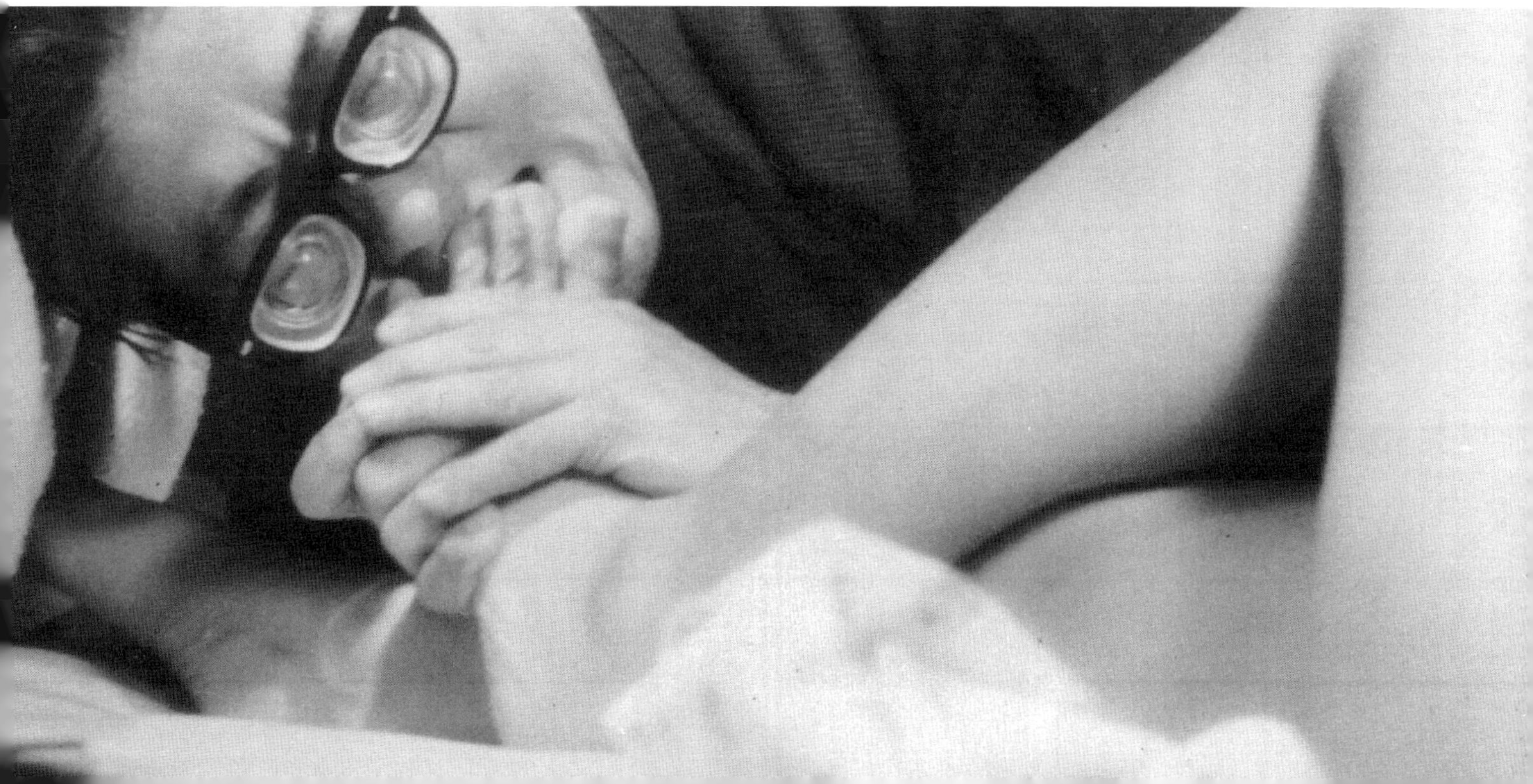

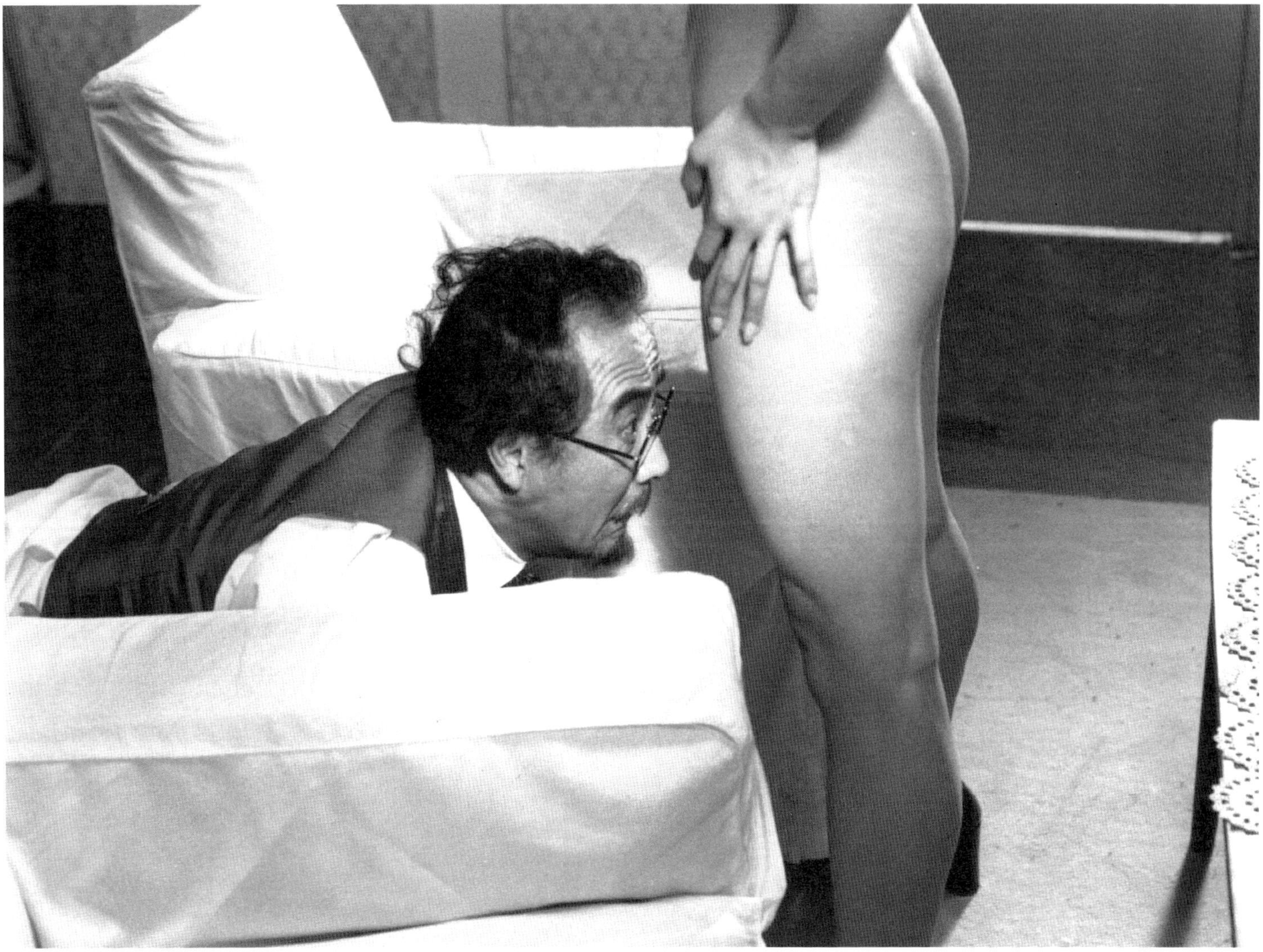

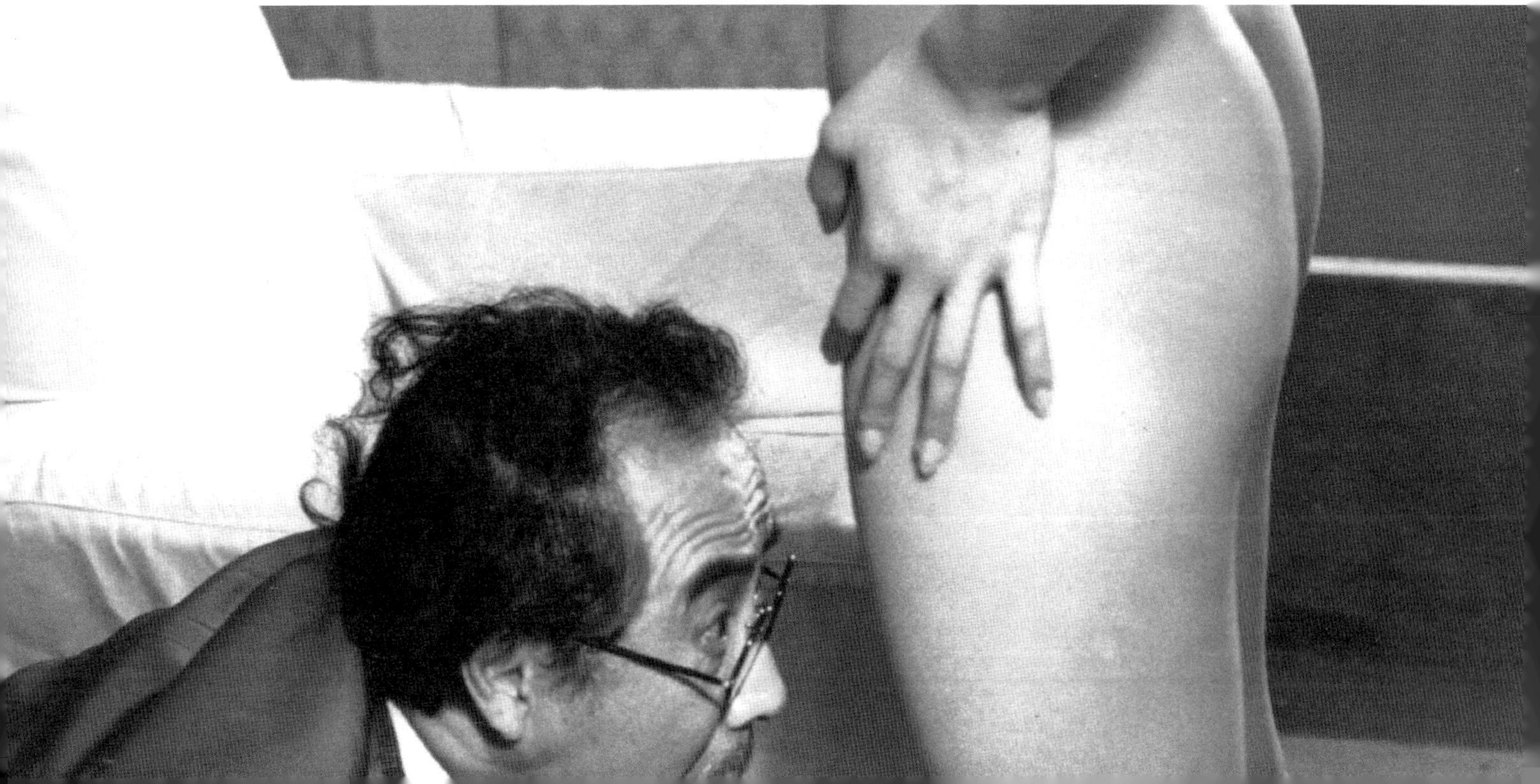

オールカラー 新宿慕秋中物語 男と女 映倫 3

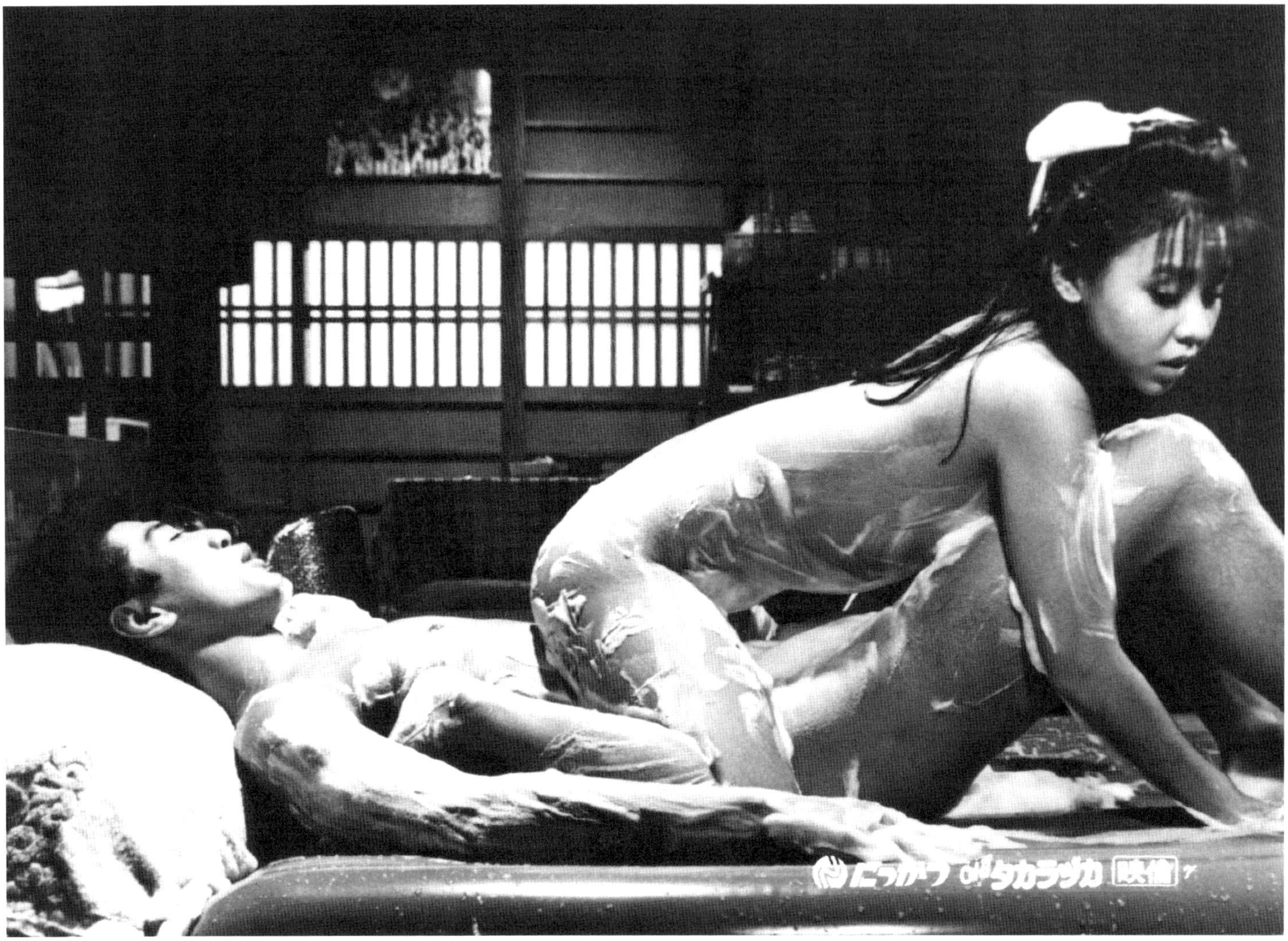

1 オールカラー 性豪列伝 死んで貰います 映倫

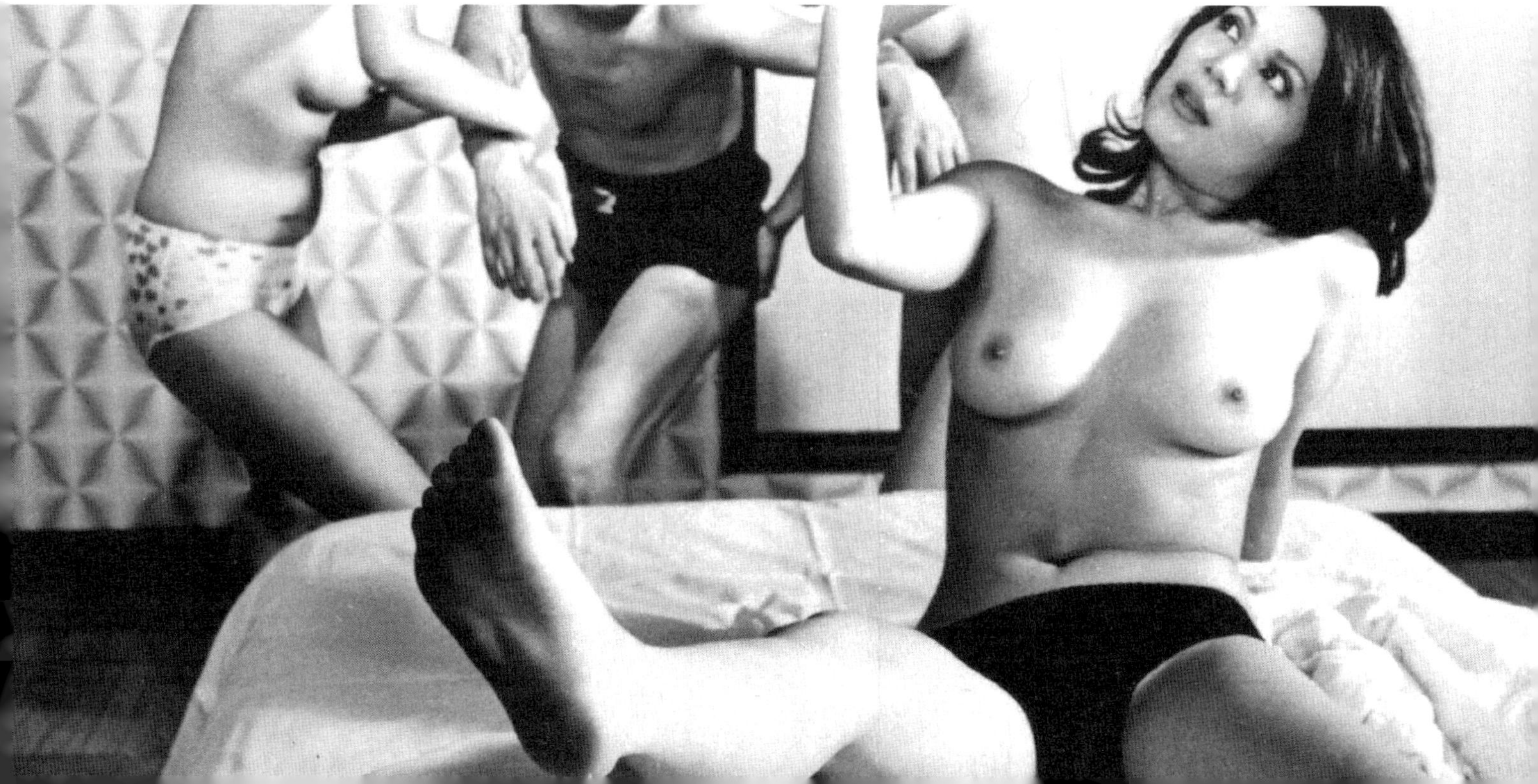

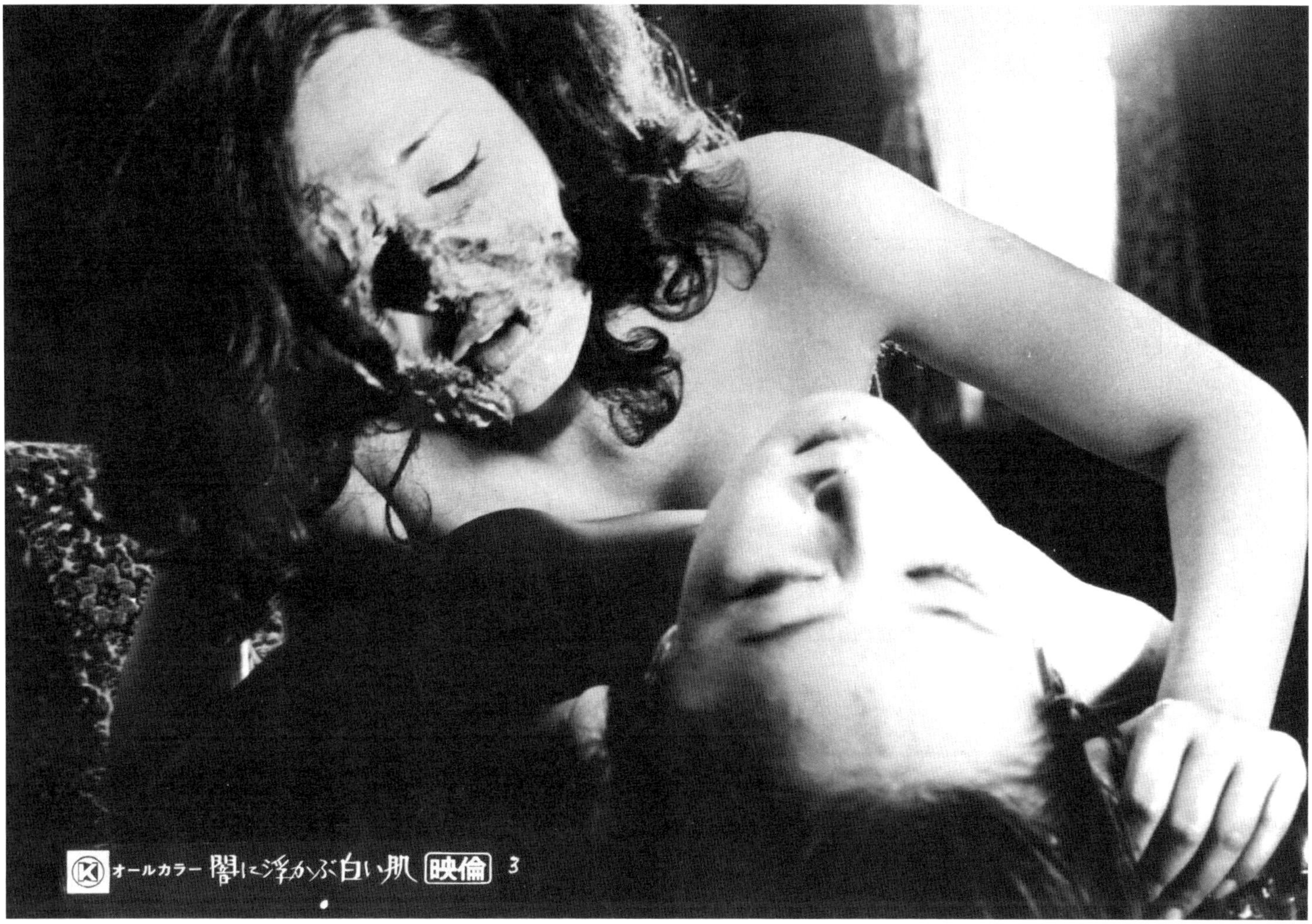

オールカラー 闇に浮かぶ白い肌 映倫 3

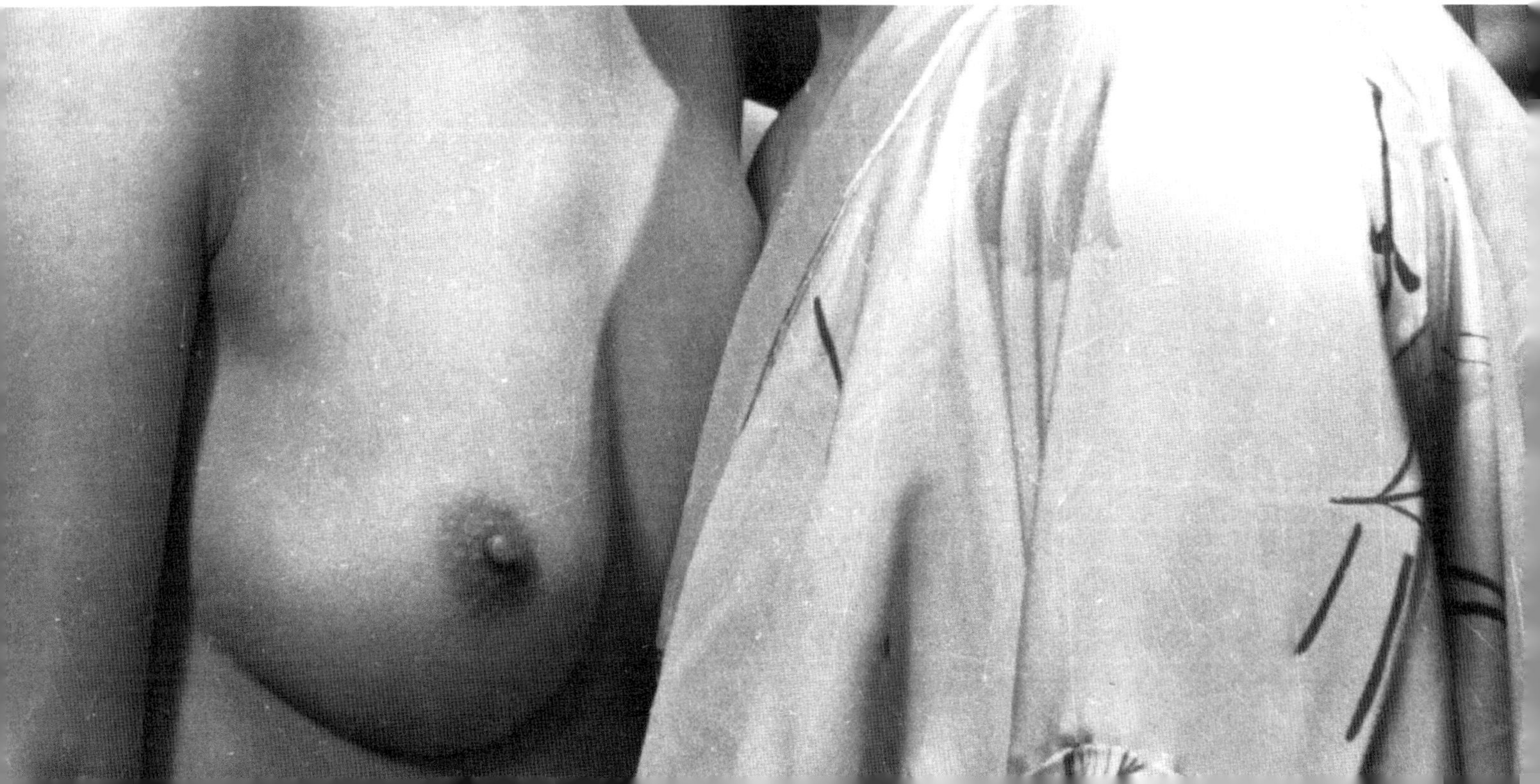

1 カラー作品 レズビアンの世界 映倫
枕探

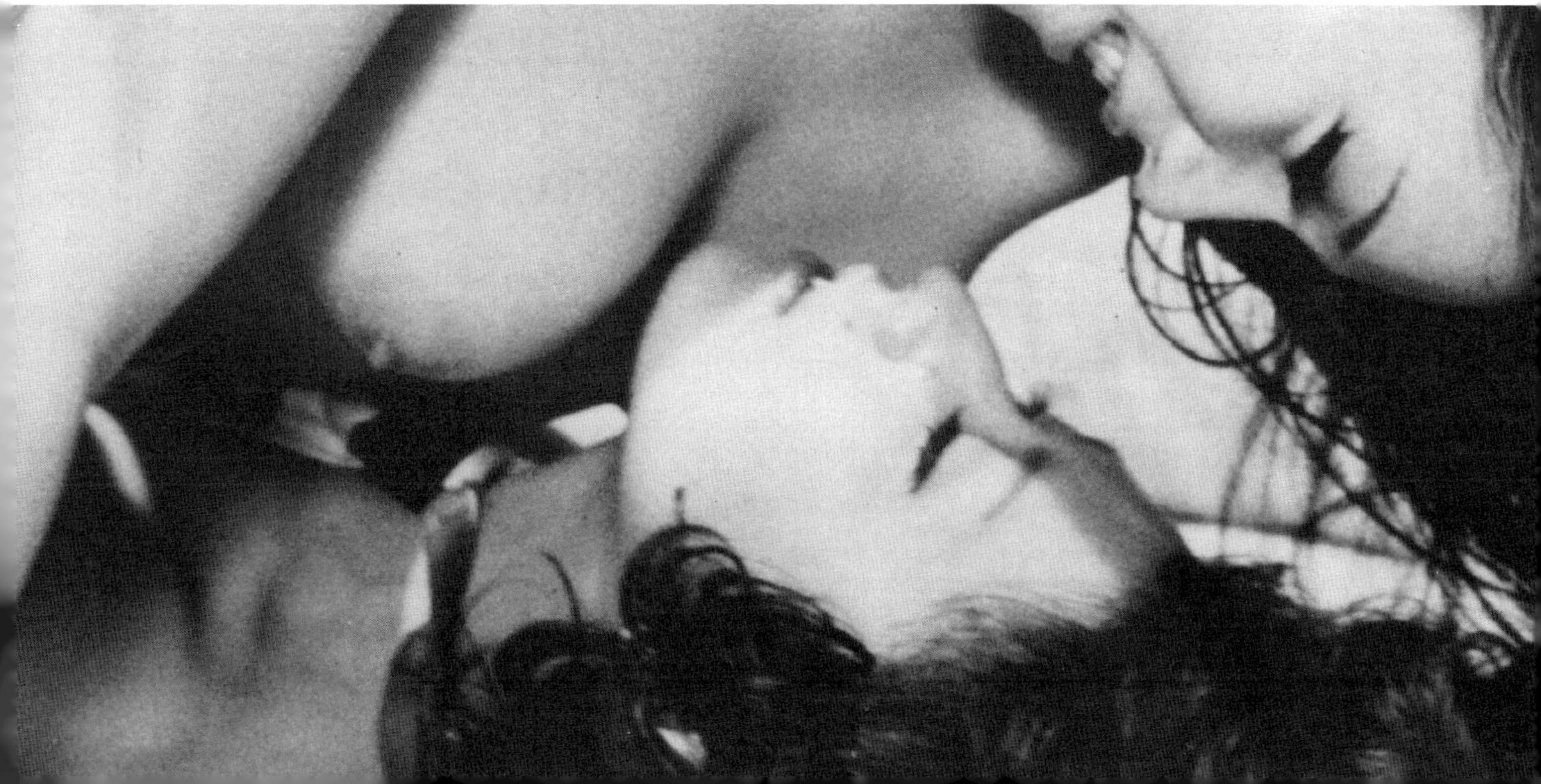

オールカラー 性豪列伝 死んで貰います

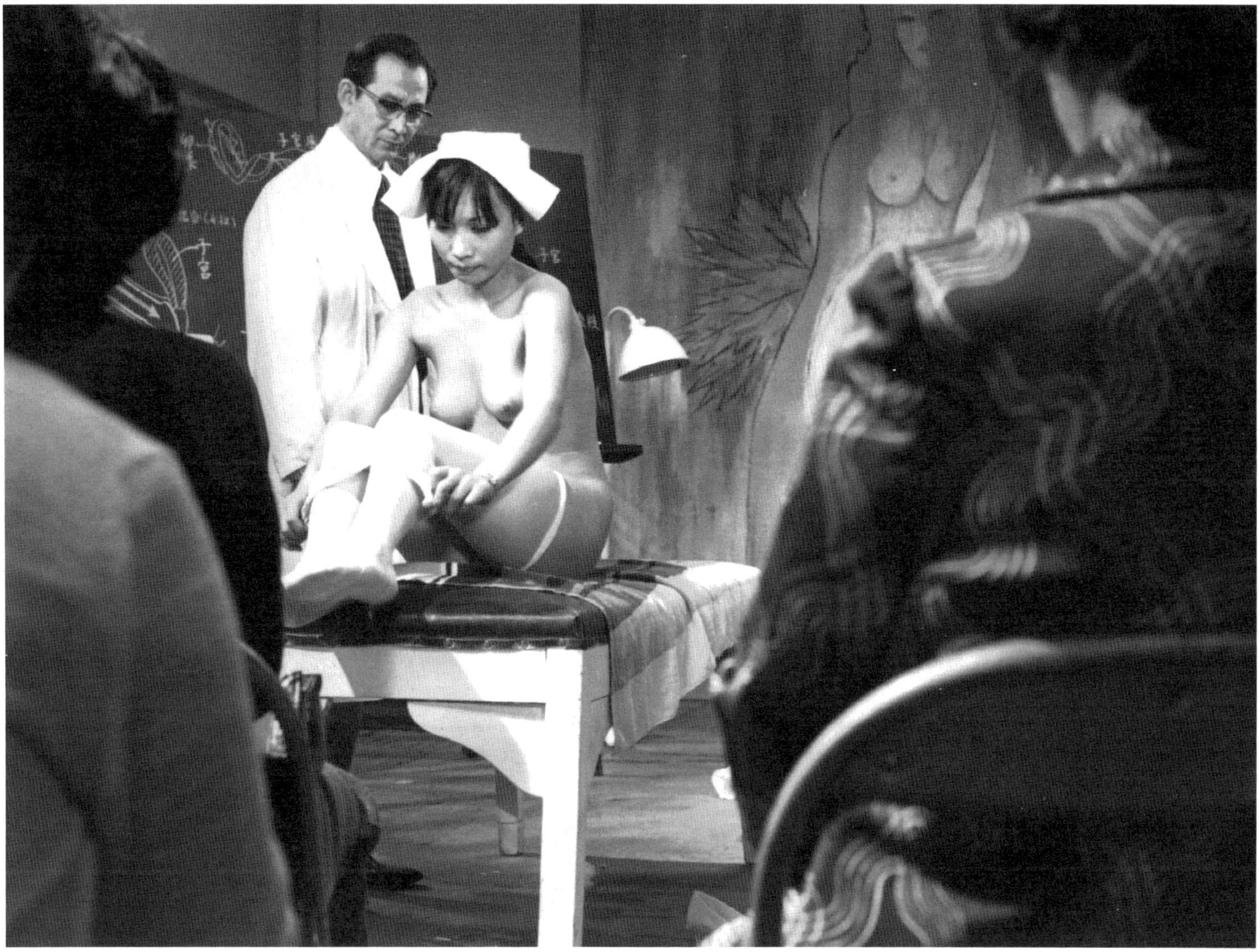

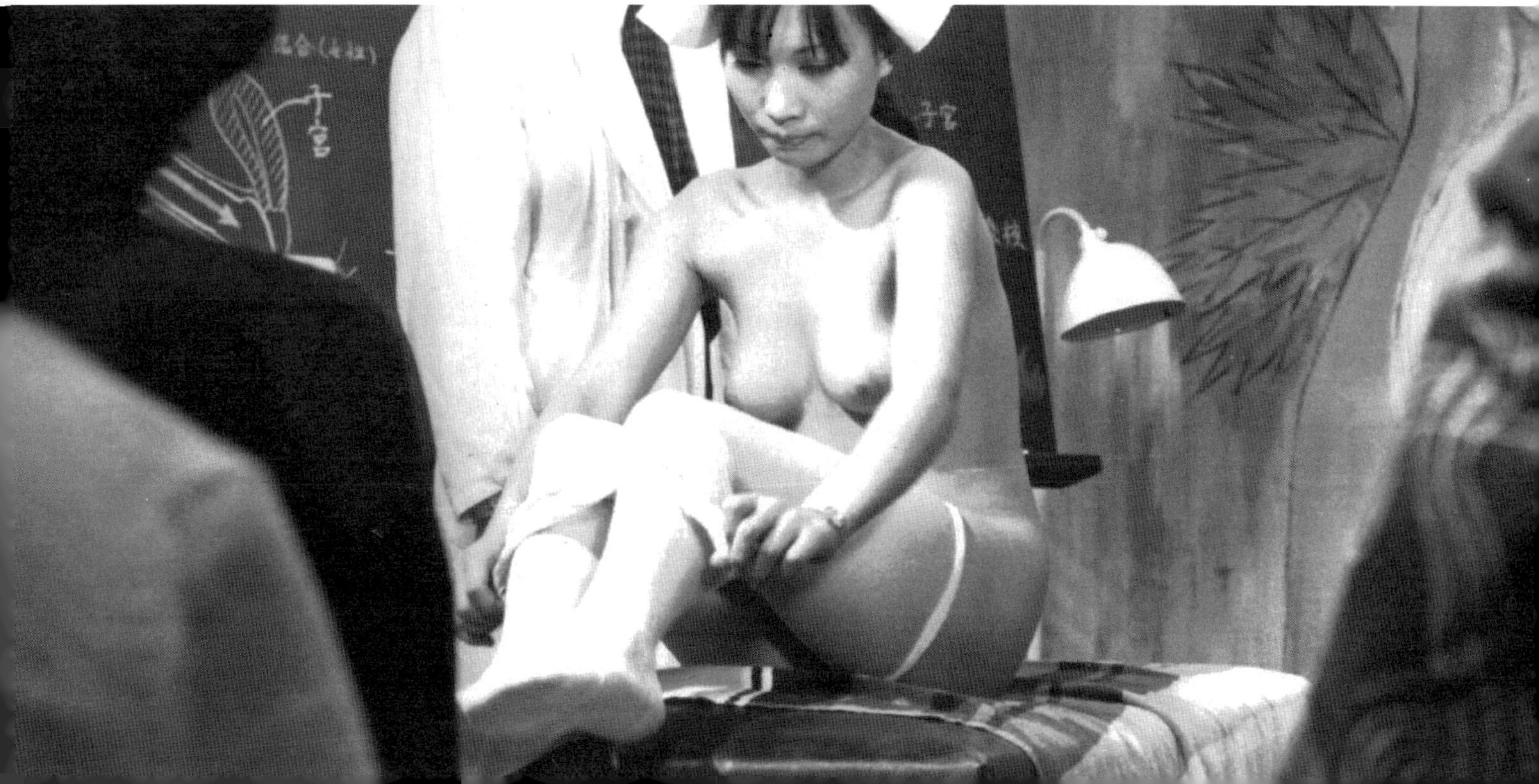

2 カラー作品 レスビアンの世界 —恍惚— 映倫

6 オールカラー 愛のぬくもり 映倫

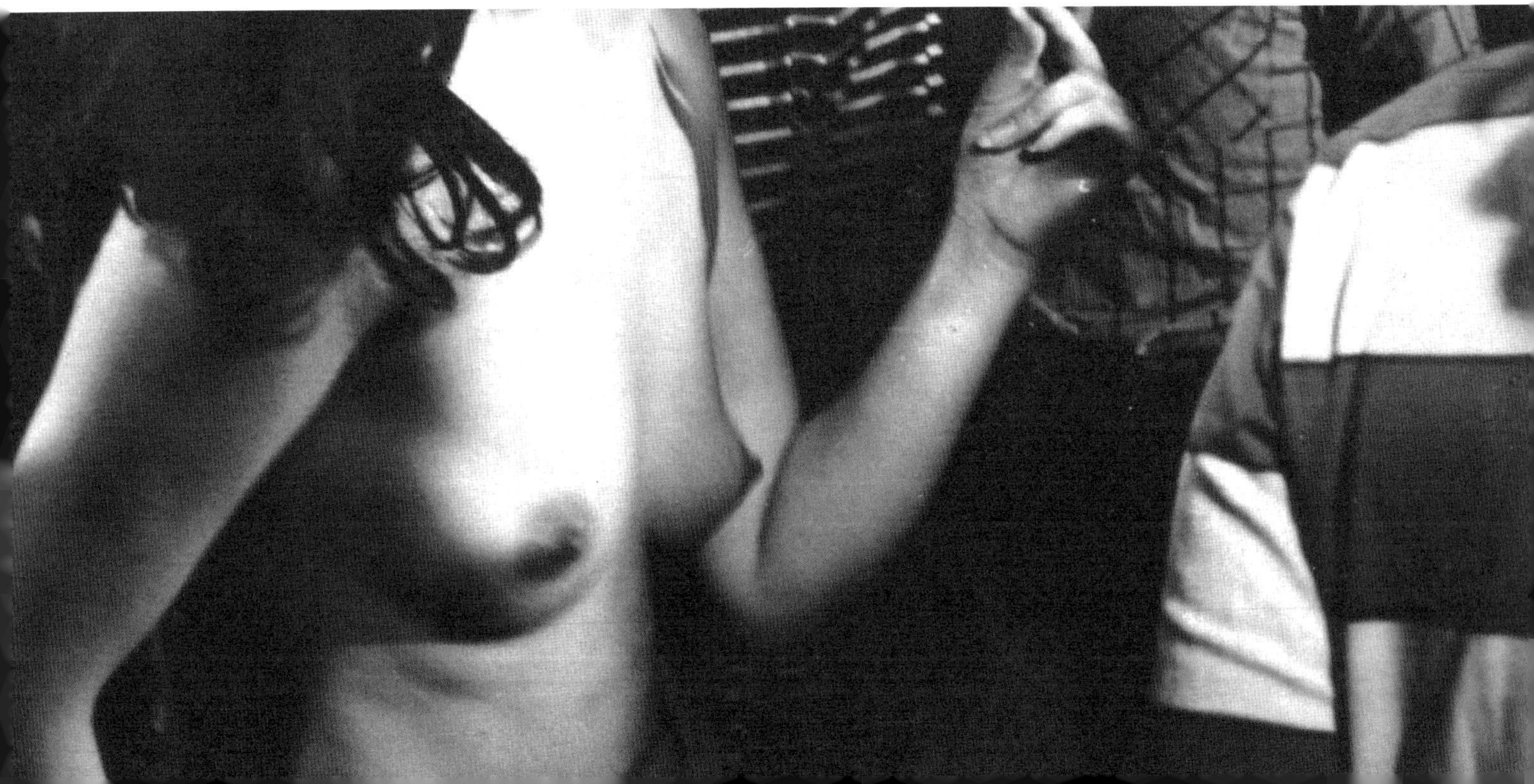

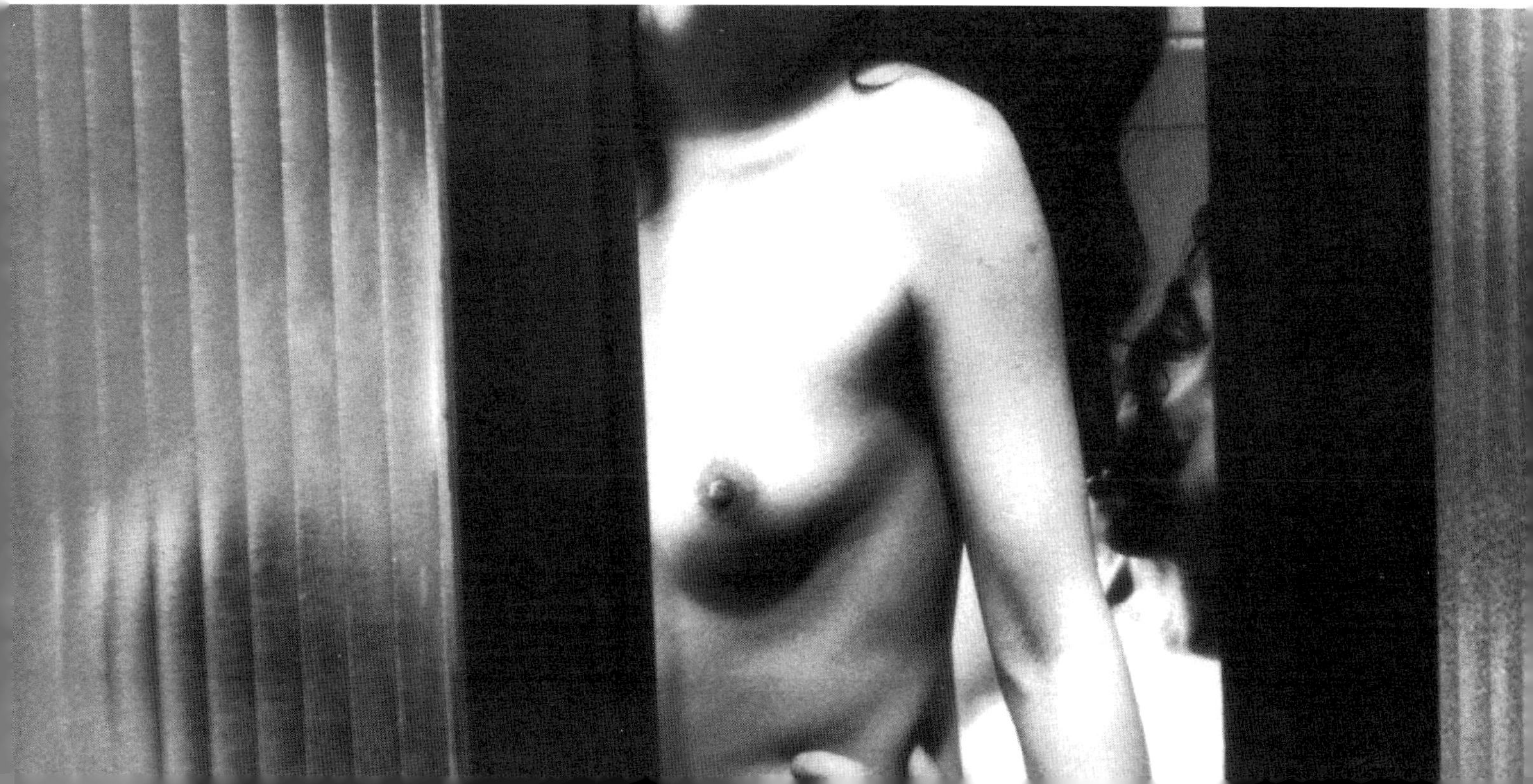

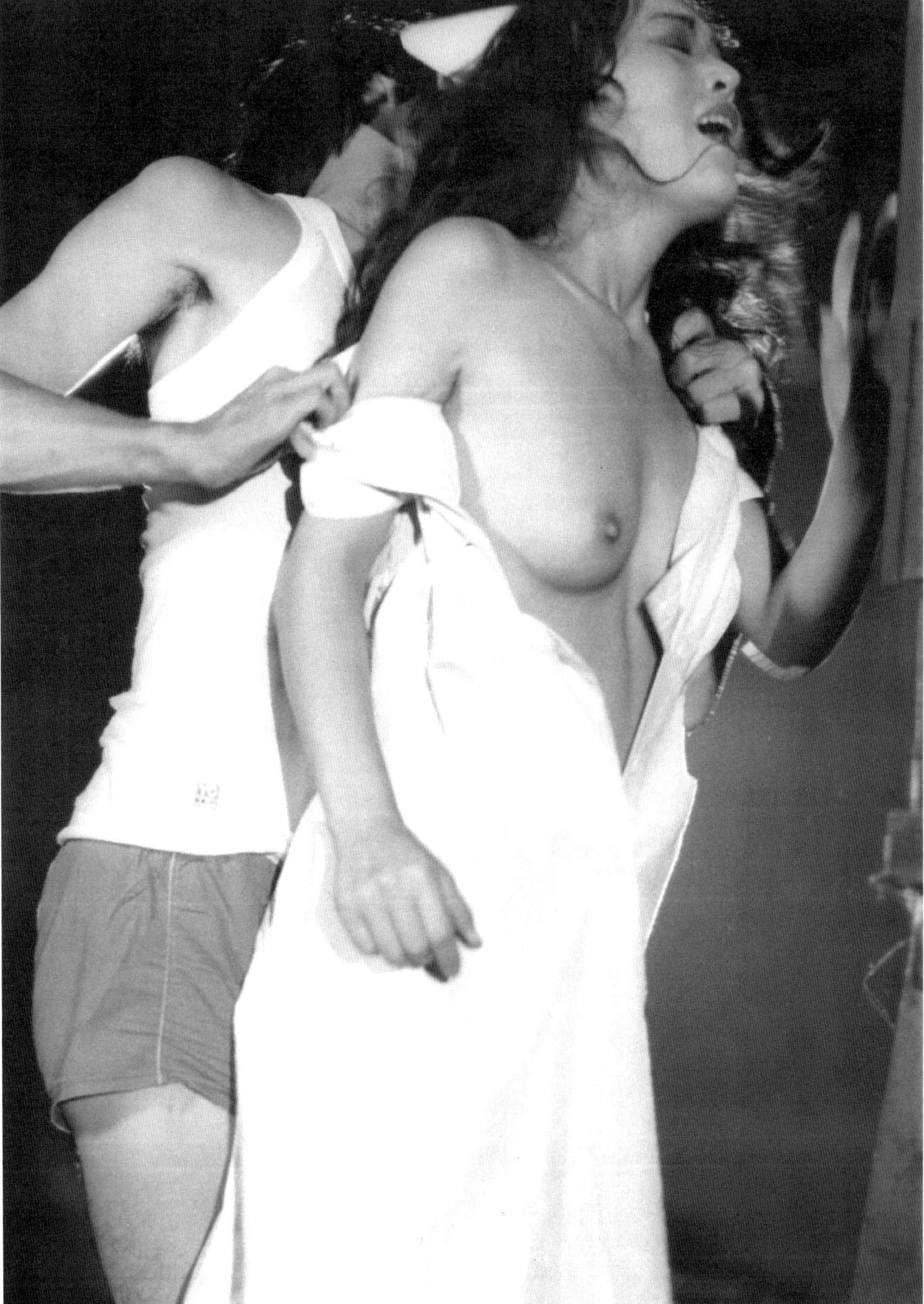

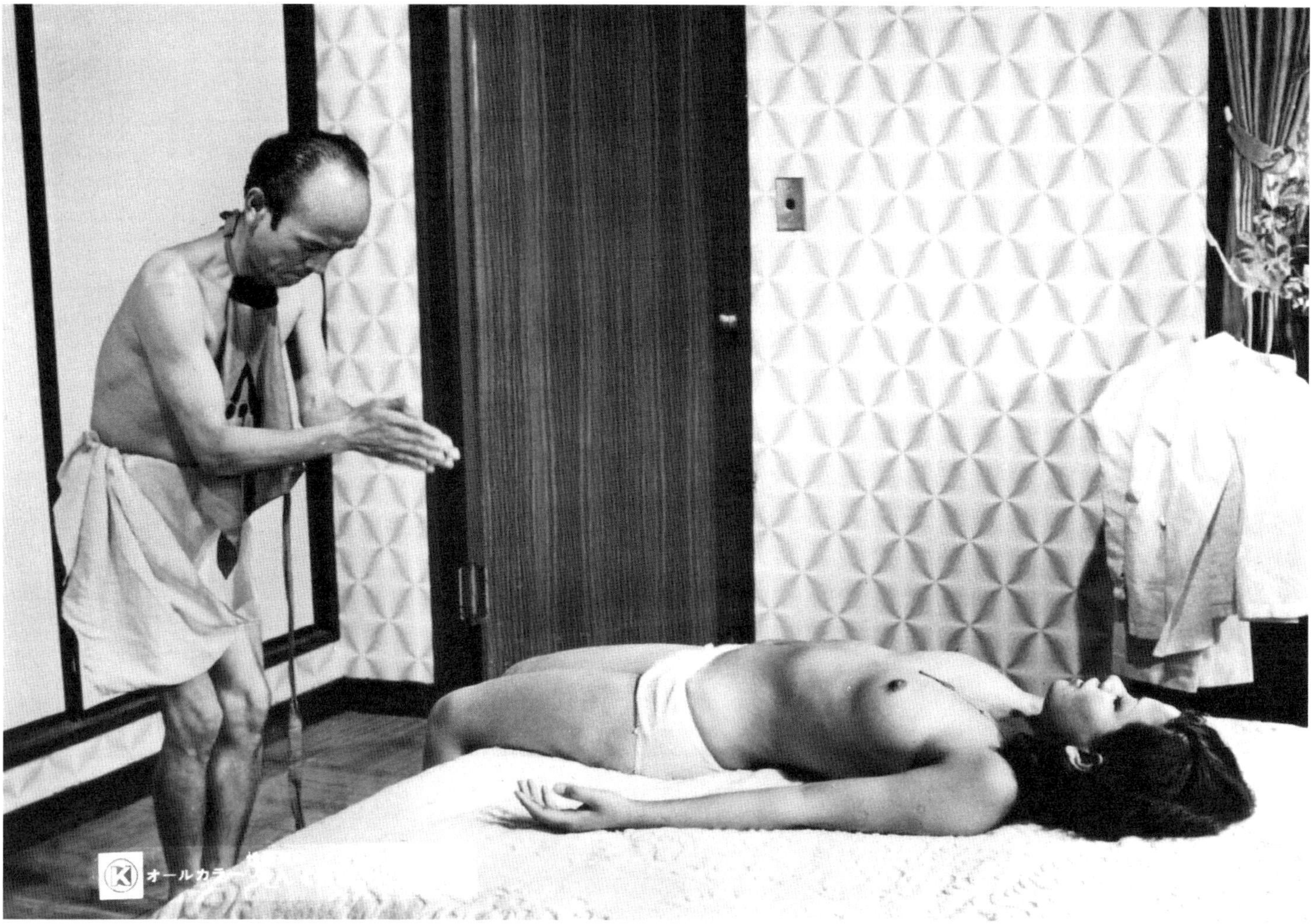

オールカラー

カラー作品
蜘蛛の湯女

7 にっかつ あつく湿って 映倫

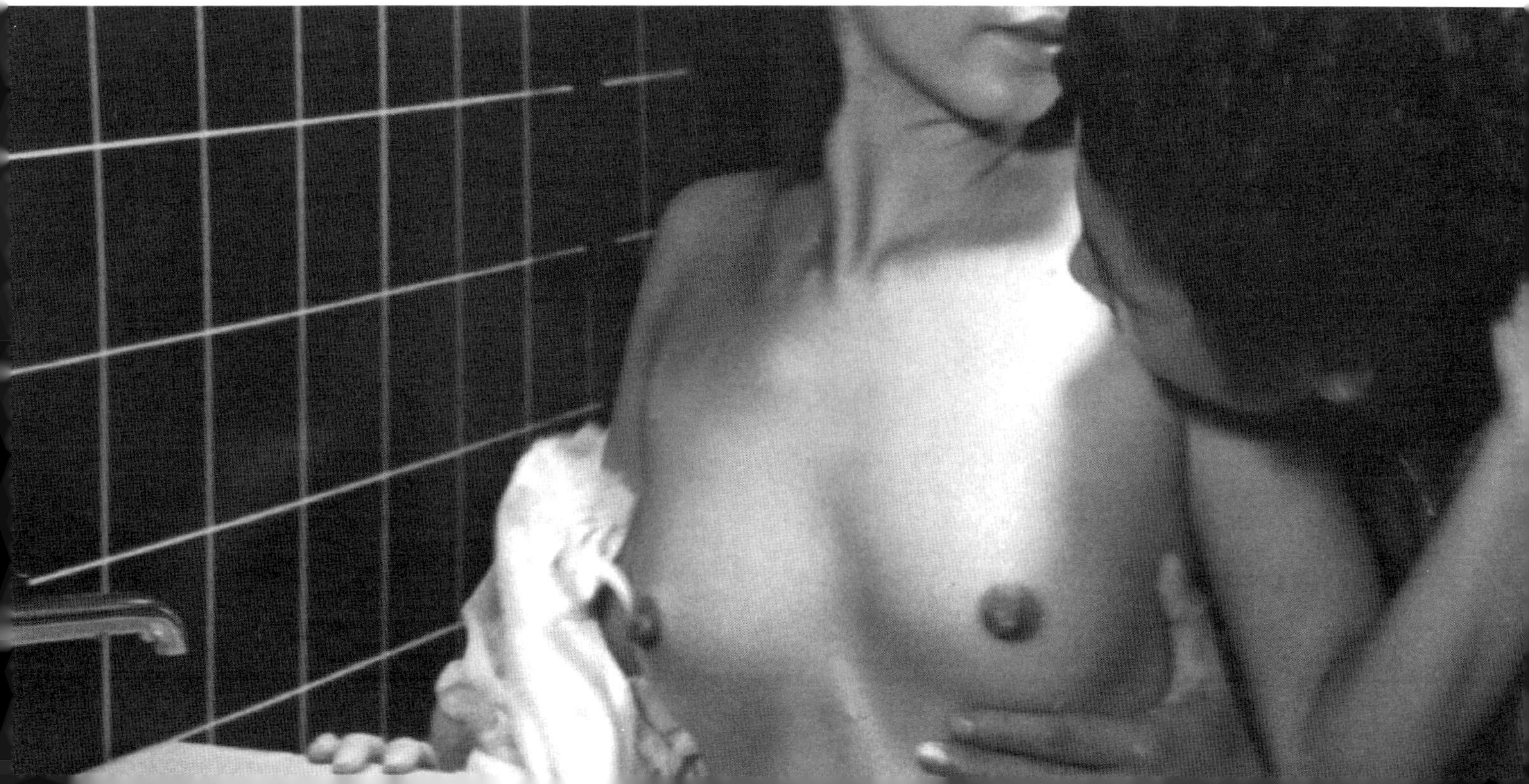

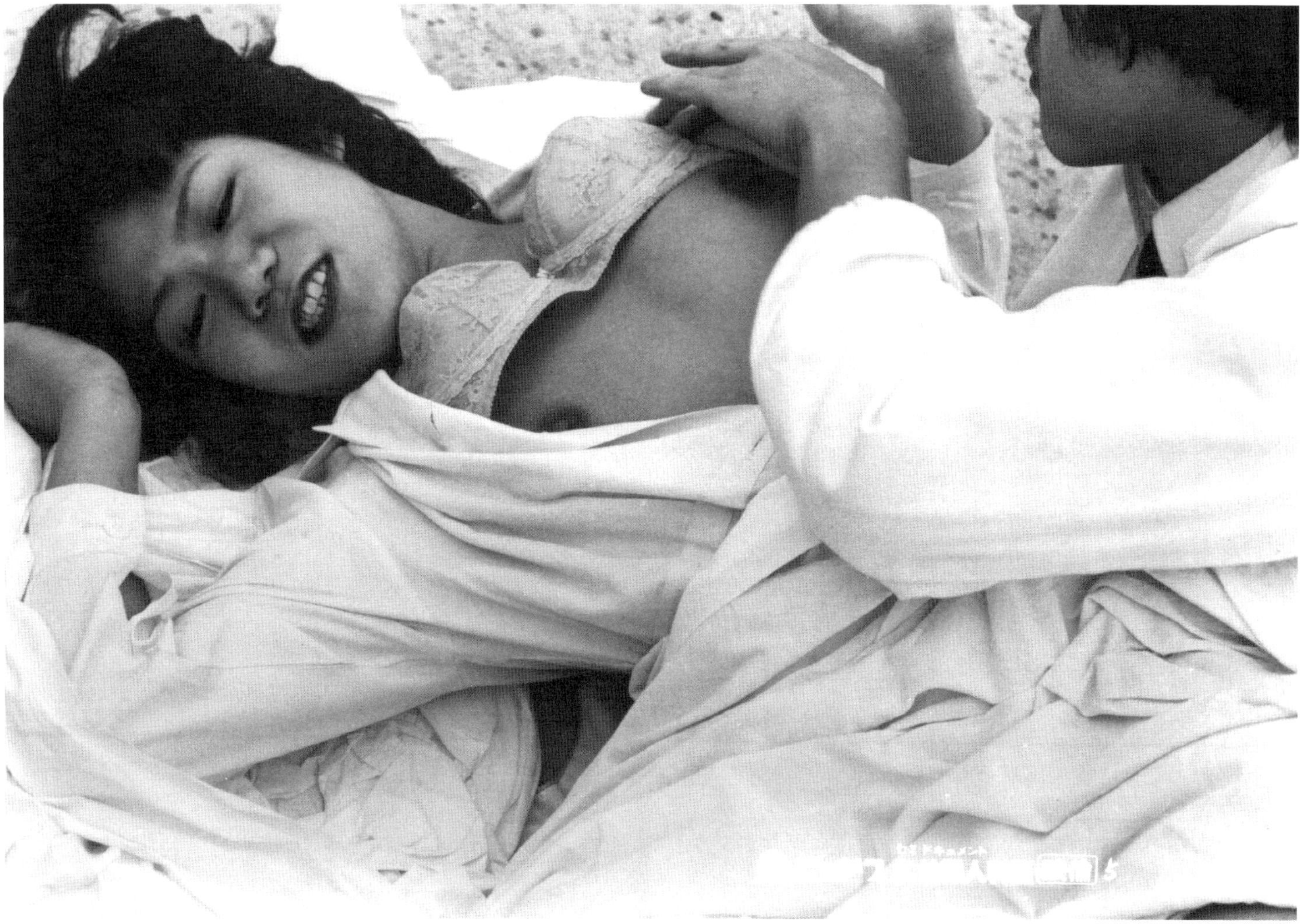

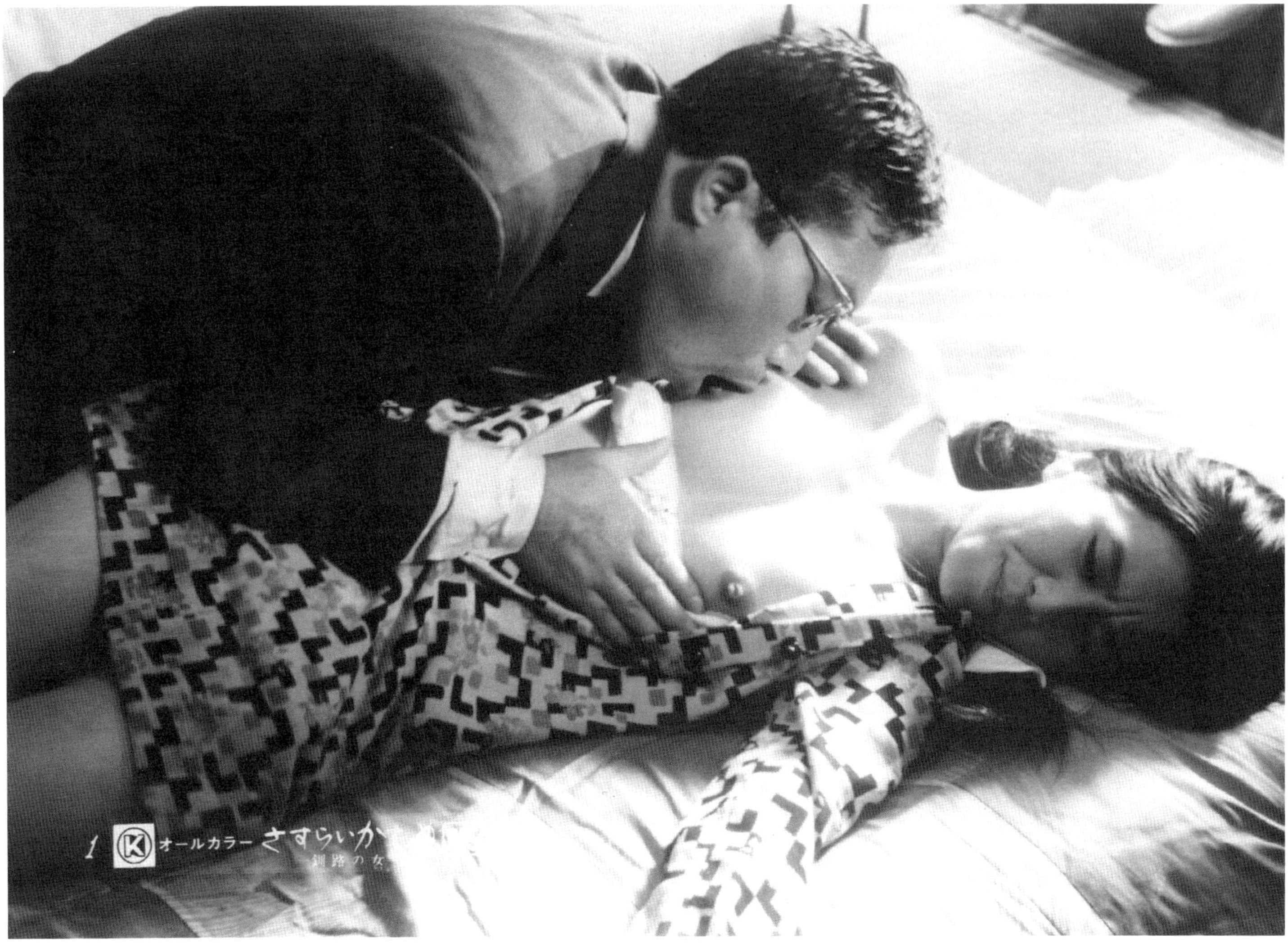

1 Ⓚ オールカラー さすらい か
釧路の女

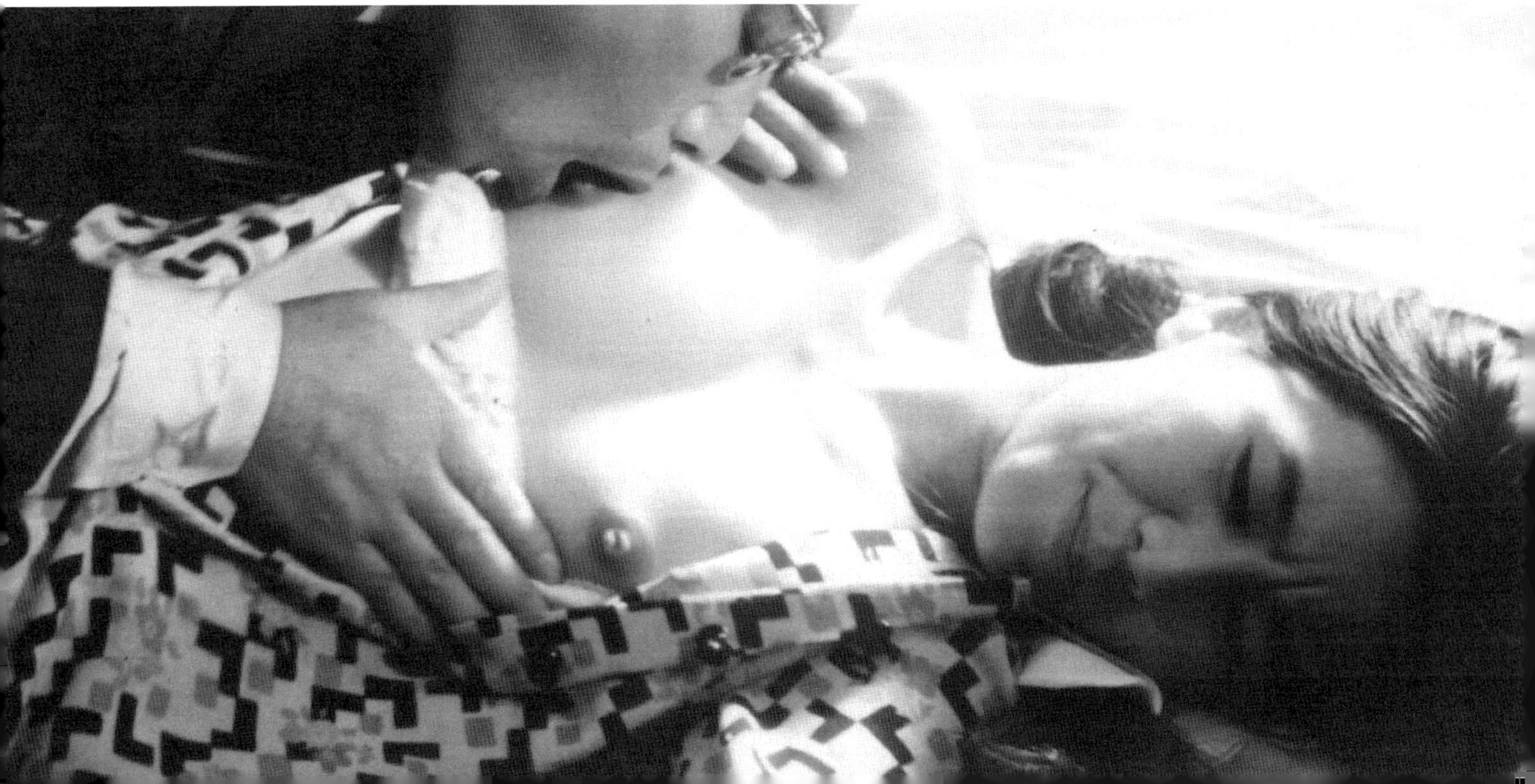

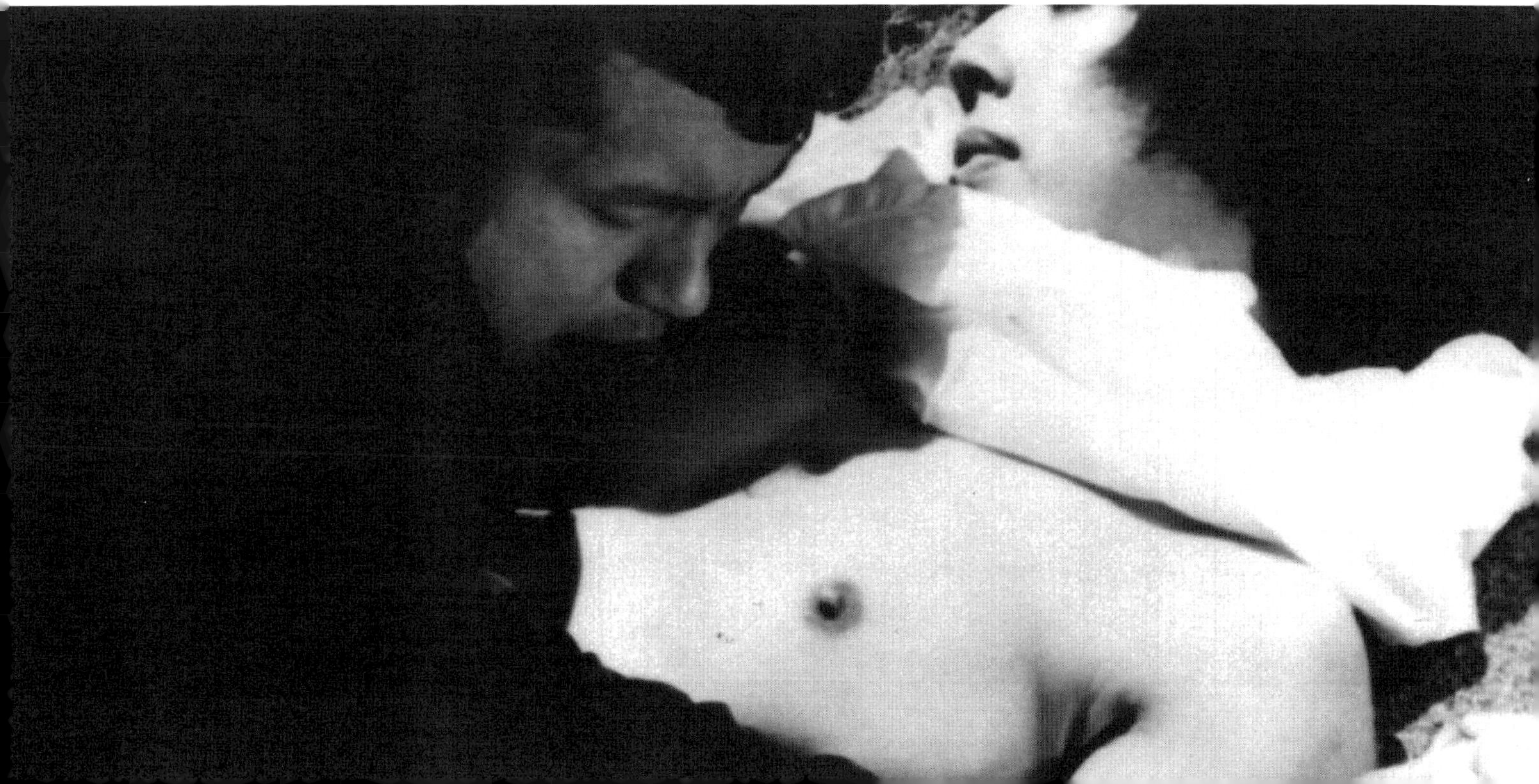

性豪列伝 オールカラー 死んで貰います 映倫

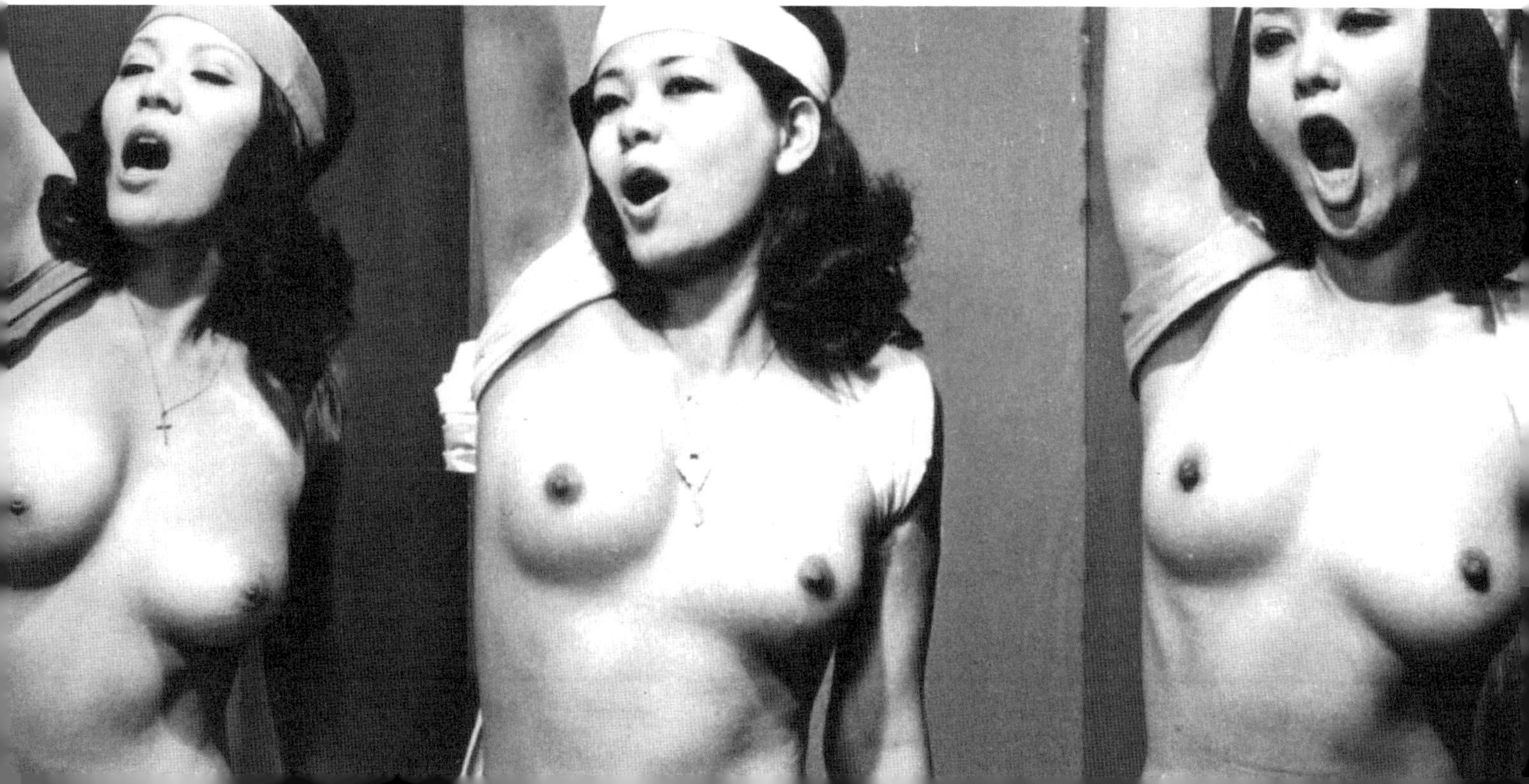

蜘蛛の湯女

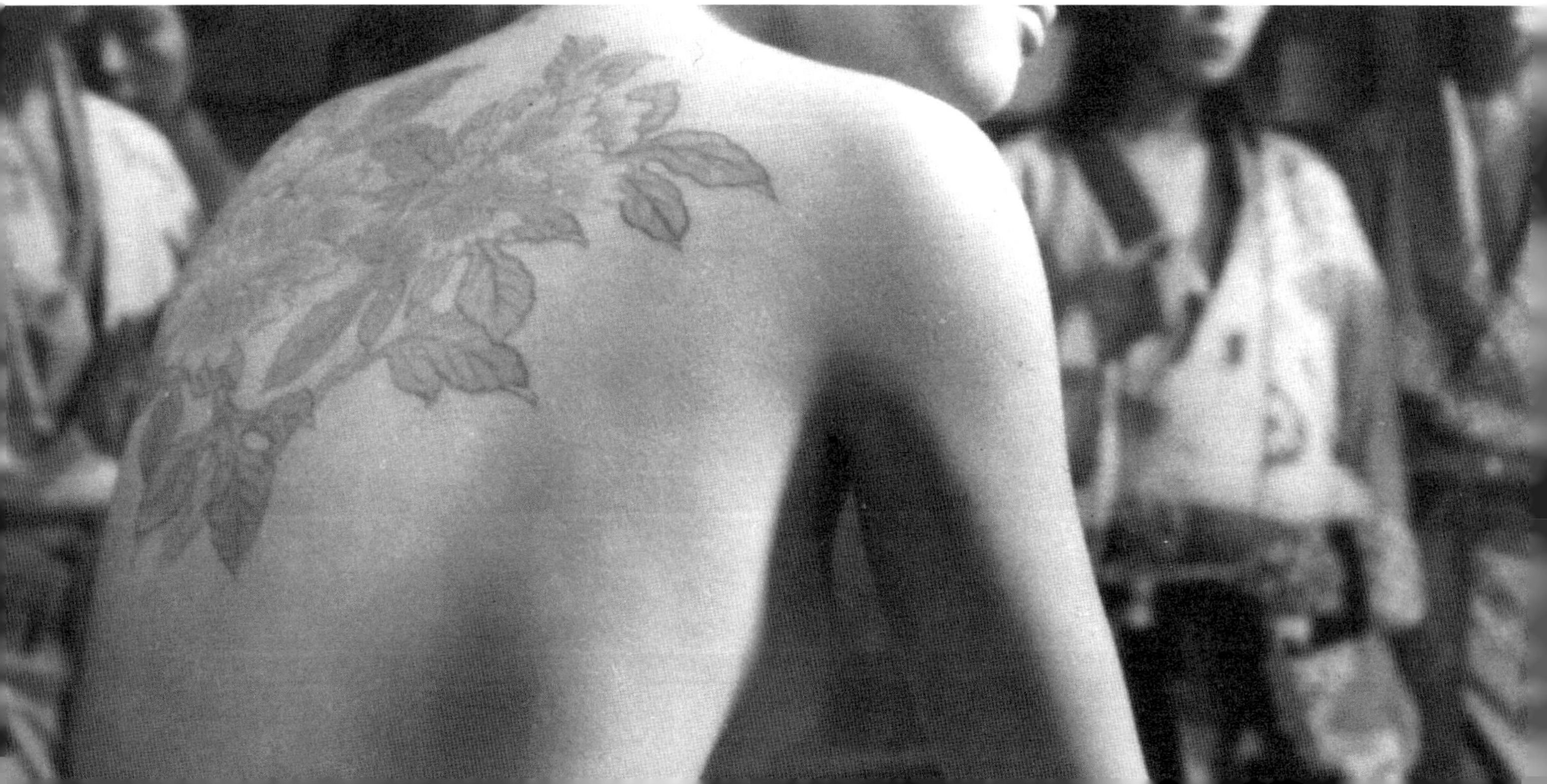

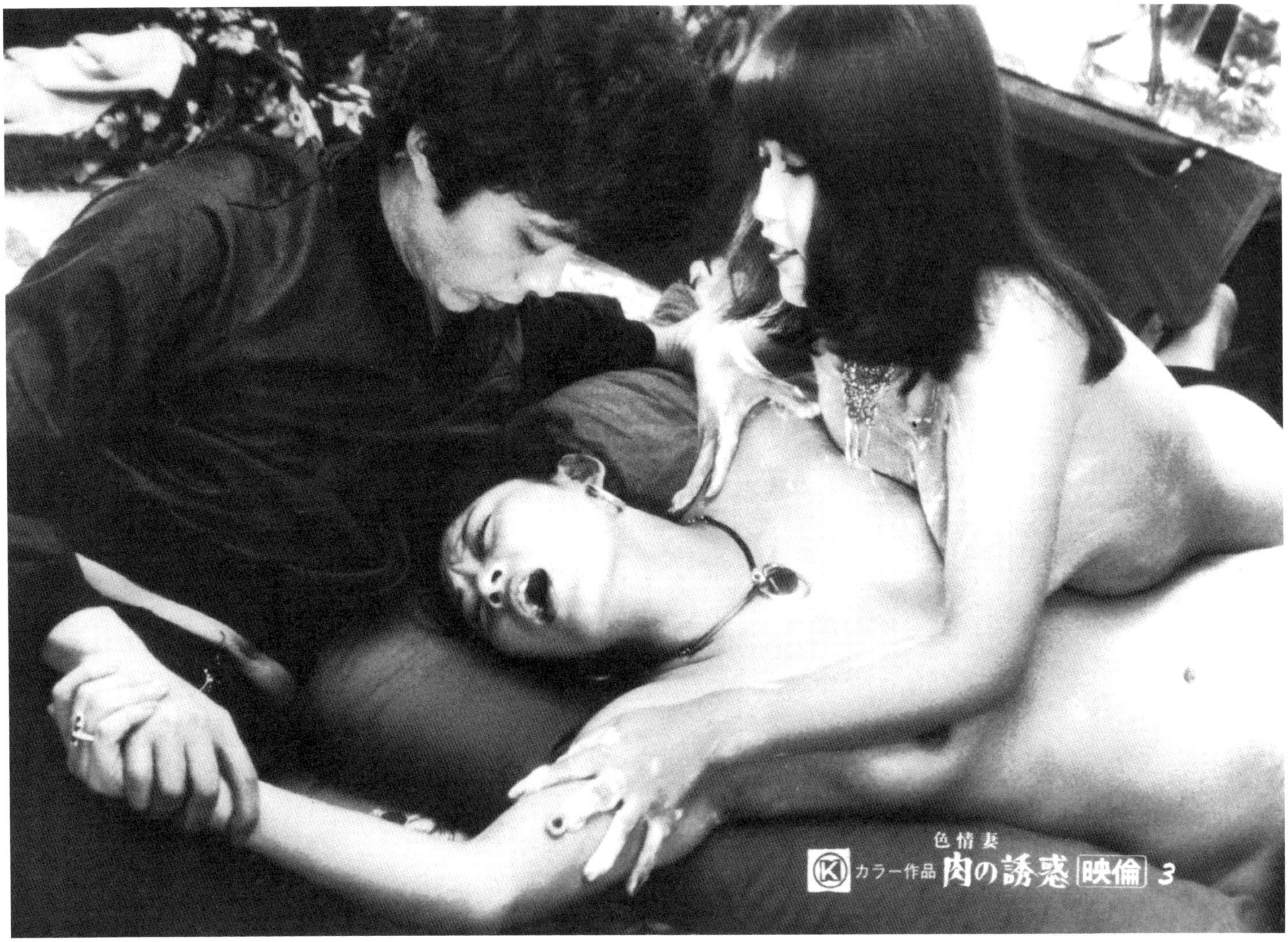

色情妻
カラー作品 肉の誘惑 映倫 3

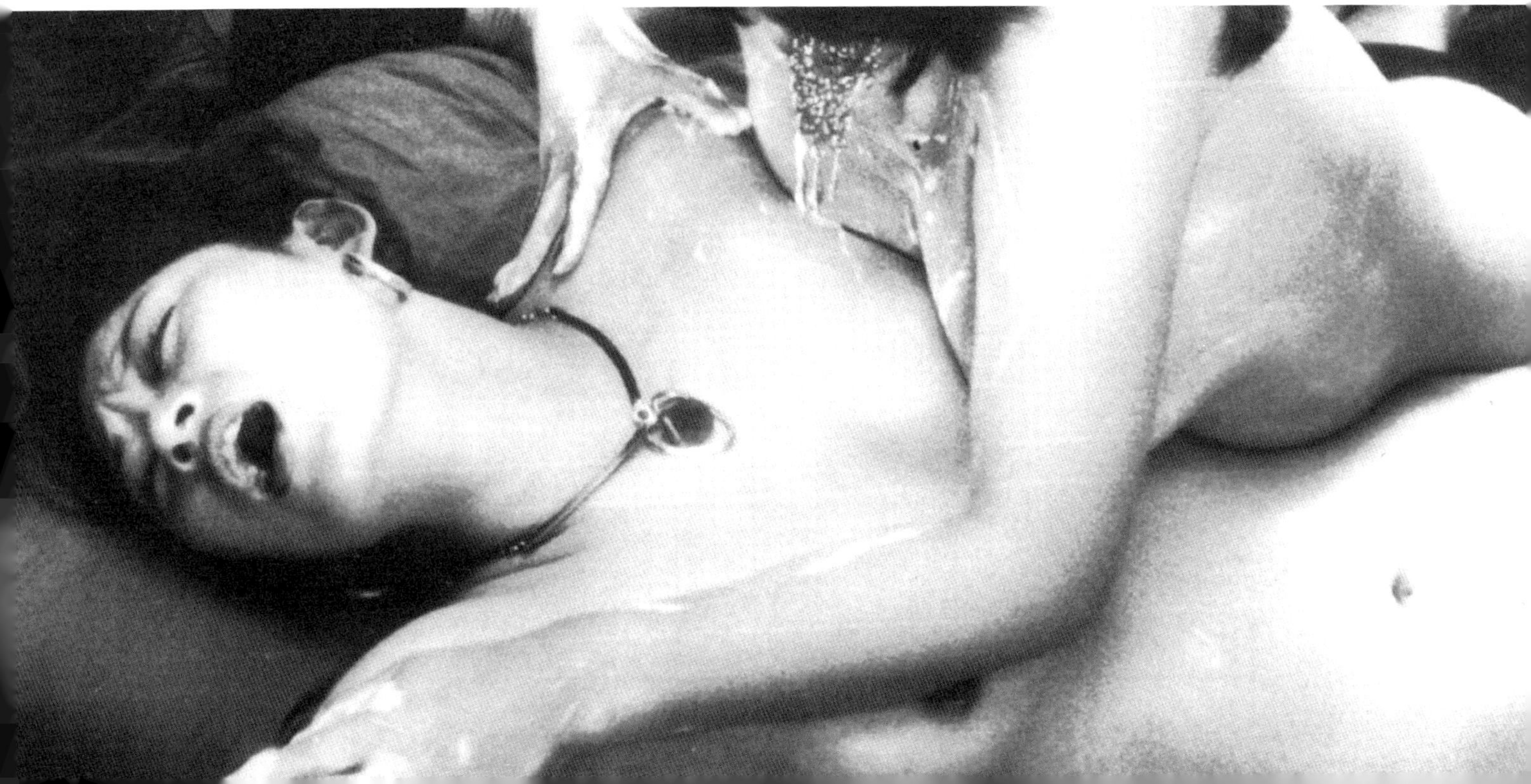

オールカラー さいはての味高原潭2

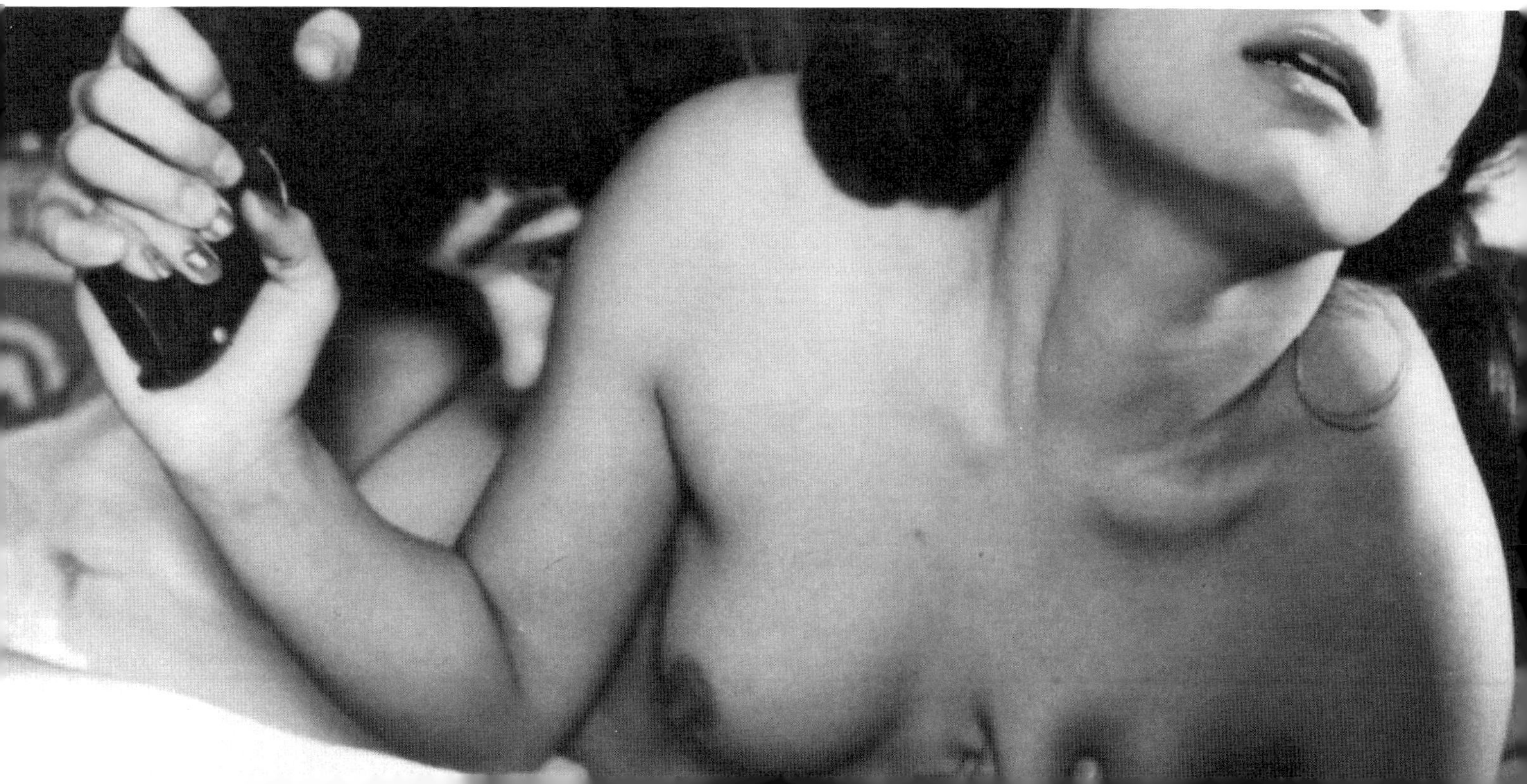

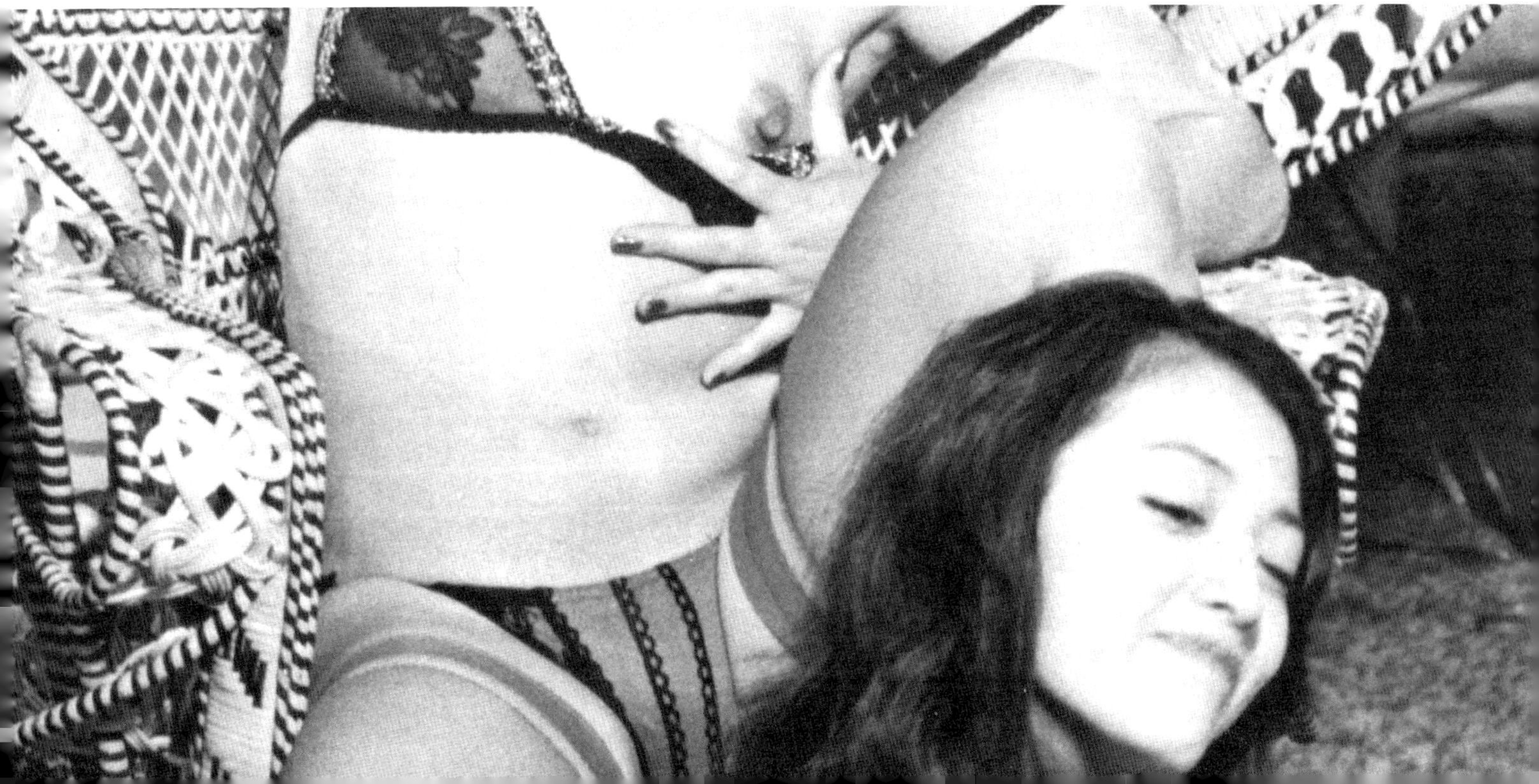

5 にっかつ ㊙強精剤 ベッドが濡れる 映倫

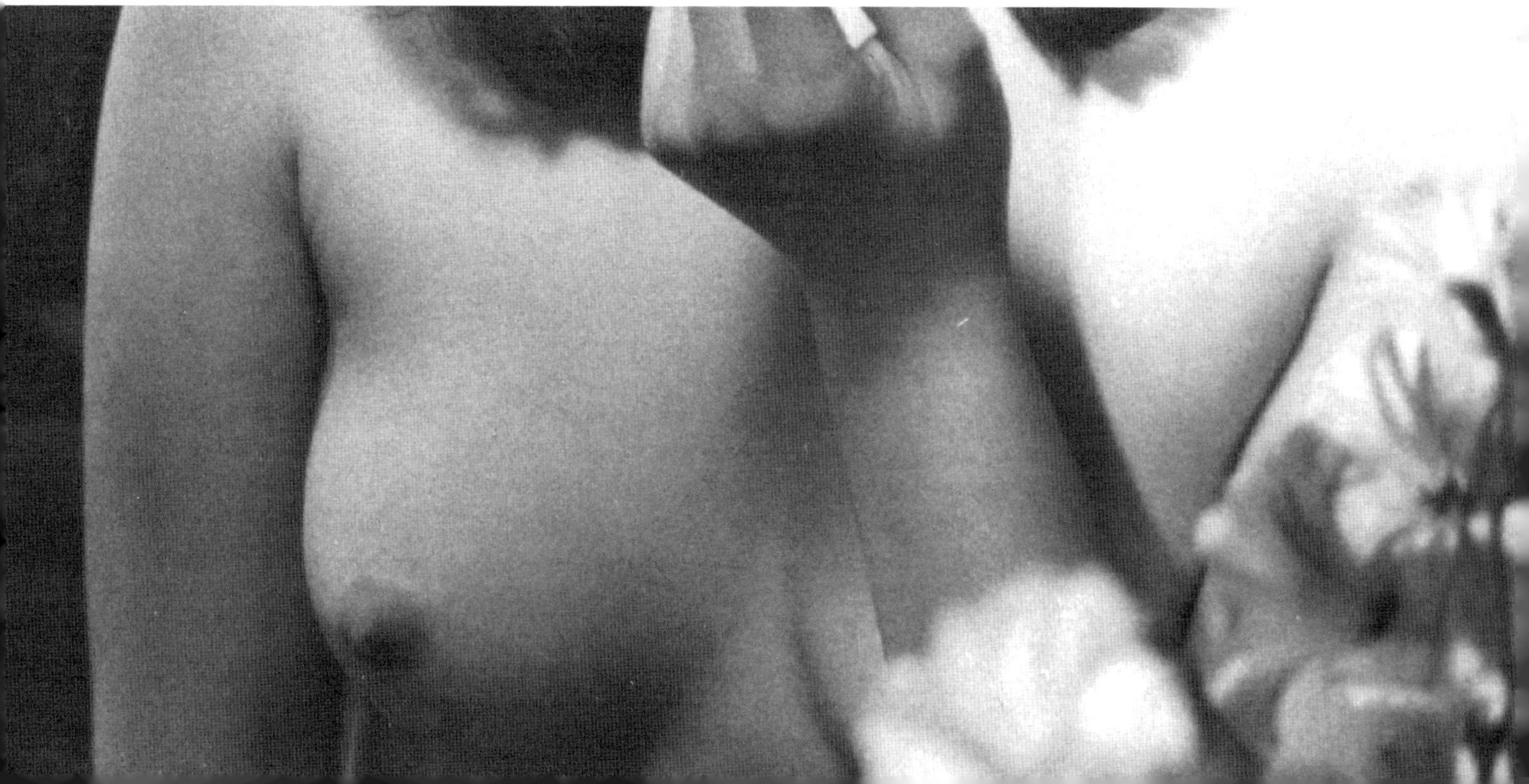

にっかつ ㊙強精剤 ベッドが濡れる 映倫

あれの匂い 映倫

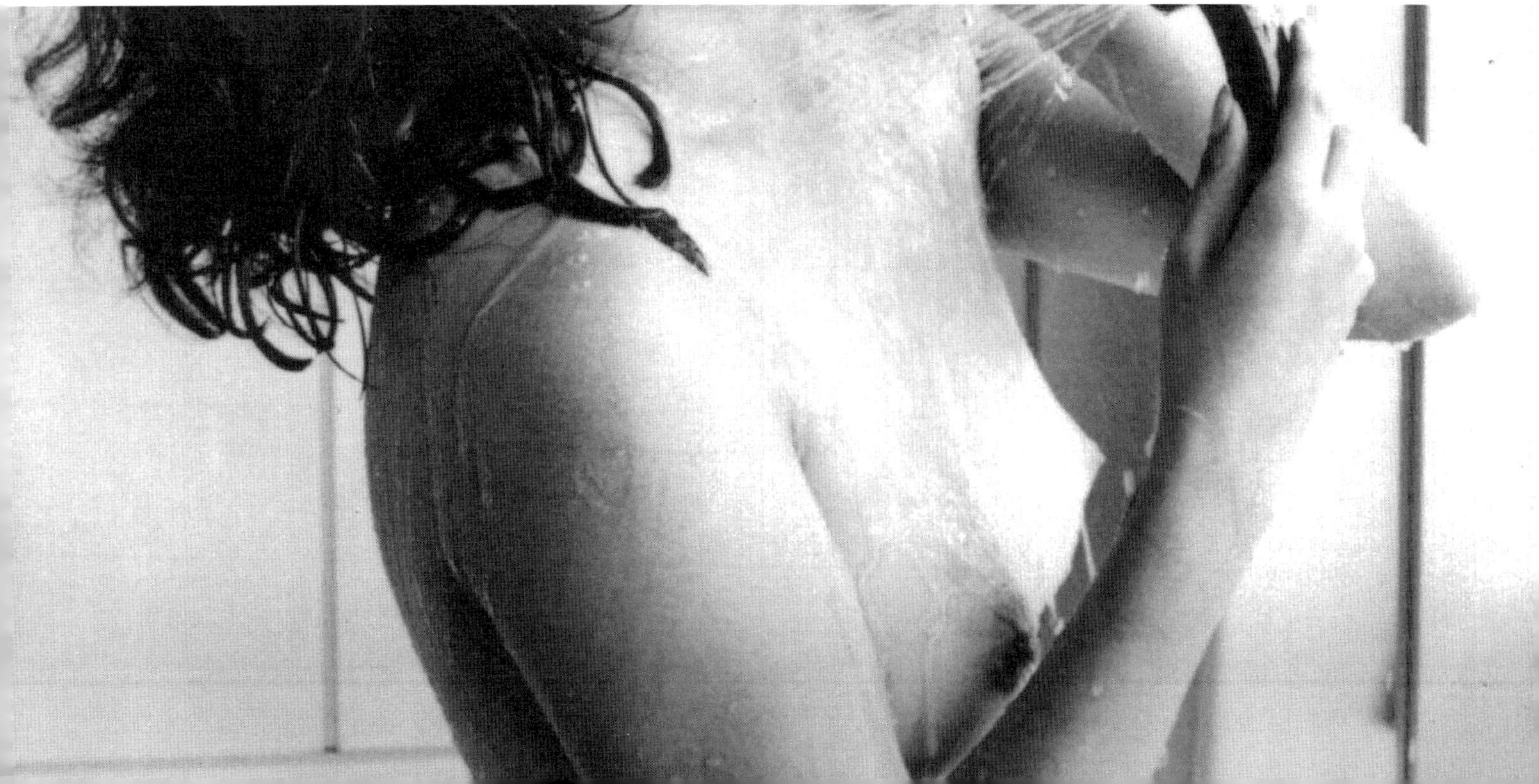

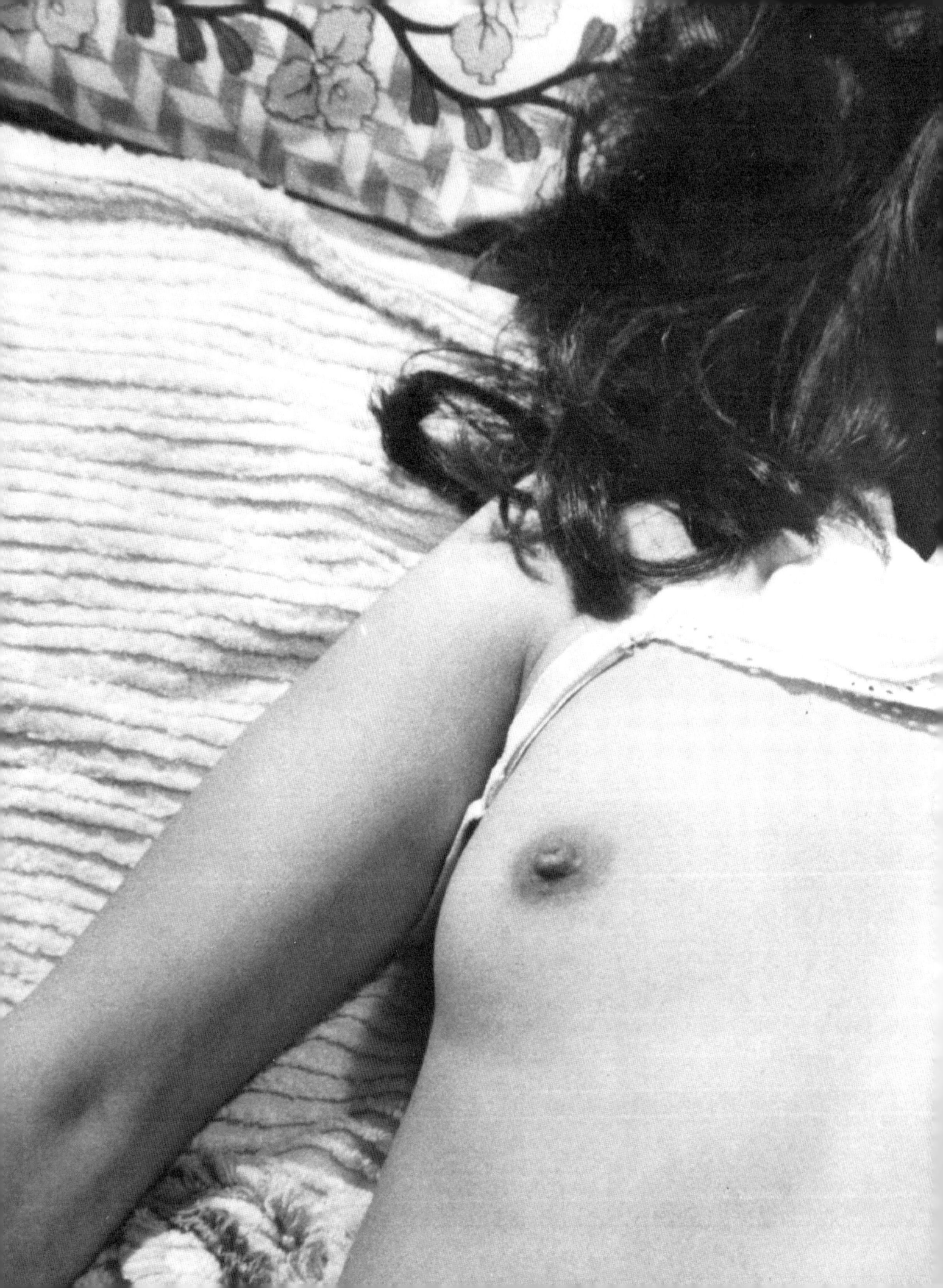

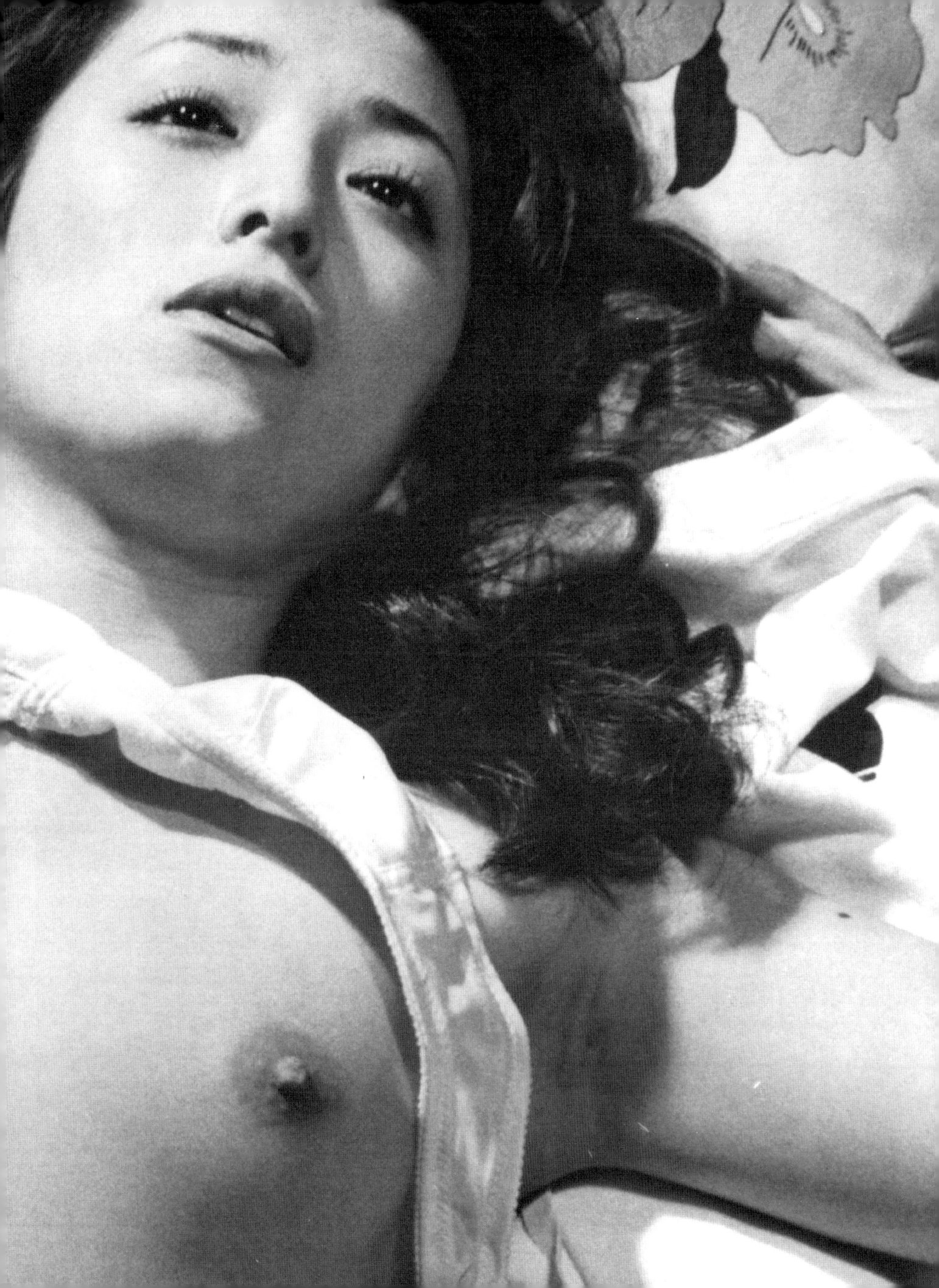

KAGAMI JIGOKU KOBAYASHI IS EDITOR OF THE "TOKYO CINEGRAPHIX" SERIES.
EACH VOLUME PRESENTS 100 JAPANESE MOVIE POSTERS IN FULL COLOUR.
AVAILABLE THROUGH ALL GOOD BOOK RETAIL OUTLETS.

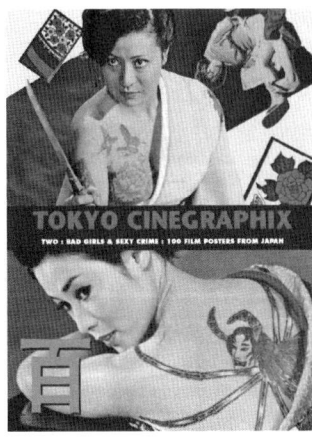

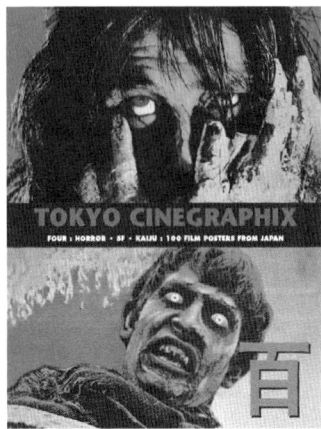
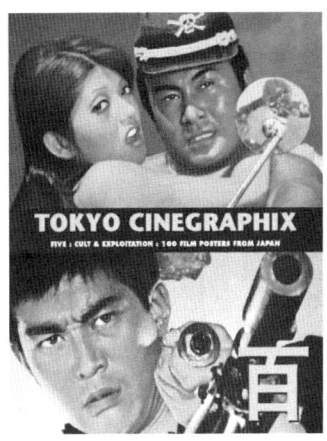
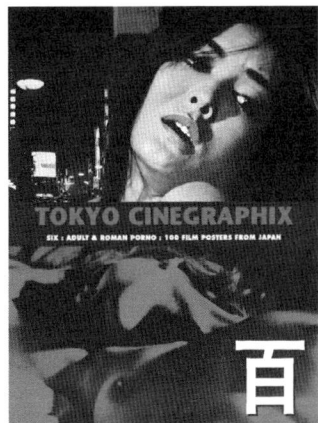
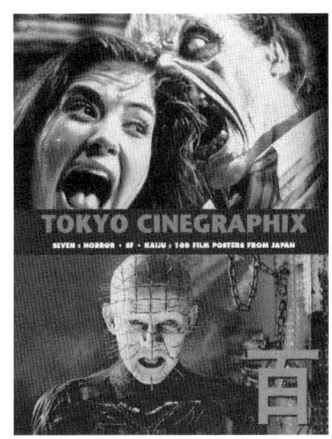

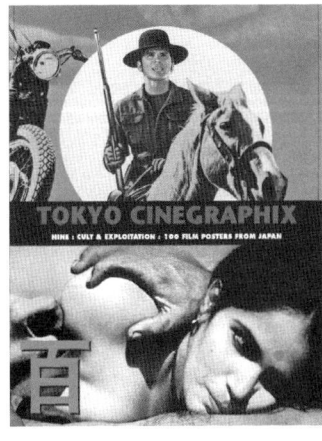
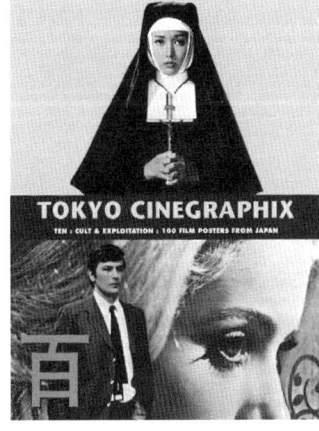
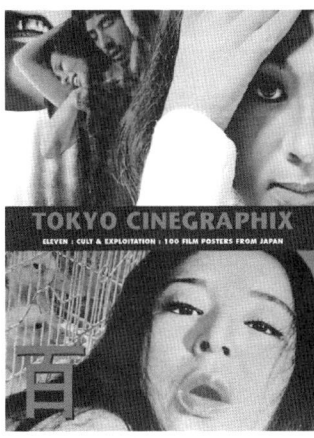